D0356956

STRUCTURES and PRACTICES

of Nonprofit Boards

Second Edition

Charles F. Dambach, MBA
Melissa Davis
Robert L. Gale

BOARDSOURCE®
Building Effective Nonprofit Boards

Library of Congress Cataloging-in-Publication Data

Dambach, Charles F.

Structures and practices of nonprofit boards, / Charles F. Dambach, Melissa Davis, and Robert L. Gale. -- 2nd ed.

p. cm. -- (BoardSource governance series ; bk. 6)

ISBN 1-58686-111-5

1. Nonprofit organizations--Management. I. Davis, Melissa. II. Gale, Robert L. III. Title.

HD62.6.D363 2008
658.4'22--dc22   2008038274

© 2009 BoardSource.
First Printing, October 2008
ISBN 1-58686-111-5

Published by BoardSource
750 9th Street, NW, Suite 650
Washington, DC 20001-2521

This publication may not be reproduced without permission. Permission can be obtained by completing a request for permission form located at www.boardsource.org. Revenue from publications sales ensures the capacity of BoardSource to produce resources and provide services to strengthen the governing boards of nonprofit organizations. Copies of this book and all other BoardSource publications can be ordered by calling 800-883-6262. Discounts are available for bulk purchases.

The views in each BoardSource publication are those of its authors, and do not represent official positions of BoardSource or its sponsoring organizations. Information and guidance in this book is provided with the understanding that BoardSource is not engaged in rendering professional opinions. If such opinions are required, the services of an attorney should be sought.

BOARDSOURCE®
Building Effective Nonprofit Boards

BoardSource was established in 1988 by the Association of Governing Boards of Universities and Colleges (AGB) and Independent Sector (IS). Prior to this, in the early 1980s, the two organizations had conducted a survey and found that although 30 percent of respondents believed they were doing a good job of board education and training, the rest of the respondents reported little, if any, activity in strengthening governance. As a result, AGB and IS proposed the creation of a new organization whose mission would be to increase the effectiveness of nonprofit boards.

With a lead grant from the Kellogg Foundation and funding from five other donors, BoardSource opened its doors in 1988 as the National Center for Nonprofit Boards with a staff of three and an operating budget of $385,000. On January 1, 2002, BoardSource took on its new name and identity. These changes were the culmination of an extensive process of understanding how we were perceived, what our audiences wanted, and how we could best meet the needs of nonprofit organizations.

Today BoardSource is the premier voice of nonprofit governance. Its highly acclaimed products, programs, and services mobilize boards so that organizations fulfill their missions, achieve their goals, increase their impact, and extend their influence. BoardSource is a 501(c)(3) organization.

BoardSource provides

- resources to nonprofit leaders through workshops, training, and an extensive Web site (www.boardsource.org)

- governance consultants who work directly with nonprofit leaders to design specialized solutions to meet an organization's needs

- the world's largest, most comprehensive selection of material on nonprofit governance, including a large selection of books and CD-ROMs

- an annual conference that brings together approximately 900 governance experts, board members, and chief executives and senior staff from around the world

For more information, please visit our Web site at www.boardsource.org, e-mail us at mail@boardsource.org, or call us at 800-883-6262.

Have You Used These BoardSource Resources?

THE GOVERNANCE SERIES

1. Ten Basic Responsibilities of Nonprofit Boards, Second Edition
2. Legal Responsibilities of Nonprofit Boards, Second Edition
3. Financial Responsibilities of Nonprofit Boards, Second Edition
4. Fundraising Responsibilities of Nonprofit Boards, Second Edition
5. The Nonprofit Board's Role in Mission, Planning, and Evaluation, Second Edition
6. Structures and Practices of Nonprofit Boards, Second Edition

BOOKS

The Board Chair Handbook, Second Edition

Meet Smarter: A Guide to Better Nonprofit Board Meetings

The Nonprofit Dashboard: A Tool for Tracking Progress

The Nonprofit Chief Executive's Ten Basic Responsibilities

The Board Building Cycle: Nine Steps to Finding, Recruiting, and Engaging Nonprofit Board Members, Second Edition

Culture of Inquiry: Healthy Debate in the Boardroom

The Nonprofit Board Answer Book: A Practical Guide for Board Members and Chief Executives, Second Edition

Chief Executive Succession Planning: The Board's Role in Securing Your Organization's Future

Assessment of the Chief Executive

Getting the Best from Your Board: An Executive's Guide to a Successful Partnership

Moving Beyond Founder's Syndrome to Nonprofit Success

The Source: Twelve Principles of Governance That Power Exceptional Boards

Exceptional Board Practices: The Source in Action

Fearless Fundraising for Nonprofit Boards, Second Edition

Navigating the Organizational Lifecycle: A Capacity-Building Guide for Nonprofit Leaders

Managing Conflicts of Interest: A Primer for Nonprofit Boards, Second Edition

Driving Strategic Planning: A Nonprofit Executive's Guide

Taming the Troublesome Board Member

The Nonprofit Policy Sampler, Second Edition

The Nonprofit Legal Landscape

Self-Assessment for Nonprofit Governing Boards

Understanding Nonprofit Financial Statements, Third Edition

The Nonprofit Board's Guide to Bylaws

Transforming Board Structure: Strategies for Committees and Task Forces

DVDs

Meeting the Challenge: An Orientation to Nonprofit Board Service

Speaking of Money: A Guide to Fundraising for Nonprofit Board Members

For an up-to-date list of publications and information about current prices, membership, and other services, please call BoardSource at 800-883-6262 or visit our Web site at www.boardsource.org.

CONTENTS

ABOUT THE BOARDSOURCE GOVERNANCE SERIES **1**

Why Is a Strong Board Important? 1

What Will Board Members Find in the Books? 2

Who Should Read the Books? 3

INTRODUCTION *Organized for Success* **5**

CHAPTER 1 *The Foundation of Good Governance* **9**

What Governance Is 9

Mission, Vision, and Values 9

A Constructive Partnership: Board and Staff 14

Board Practices: Oversight, Resources,
and Planning 15

CHAPTER 2 *Building a Board* **29**

Size 29

Composition 31

Cultivation and Recruitment 33

Election 36

Orientation 36

Term Limits and Re-Election 38

Turnover as Revitalization 42

CHAPTER 3 *Board Leadership* **45**

Roles and Responsibilities of the Chair
and the Chief Executive 46

Characteristics of Effective Leaders 50

Development of New Leadership 51

CHAPTER 4 *Committee Structure* **57**

Committees and Task Forces 57

Essential Standing Committees 60

Advisory Councils and Emeritus Positions 64

Evaluating and Restructuring Committees
and Task Forces 66

CHAPTER 5 *Board Meetings* **69**
  Planning the Meeting 70
  Preparing for the Meeting 73
  Chairing the Meeting 78
  Attending the Meeting 80
  Meeting Minutes 82
  Executive Sessions 83
  Evaluating the Meeting 85
  Retreats 86

CHAPTER 6 *Board Dynamics* **89**
  Building Trust through Open Communication 89
  Moving from Forming to Performing 92
  Toning Down Dissonance 96

CONCLUSION *Toward a Better Board* **99**
  Six Things to Remember 99

APPENDIX I *Sample Job Descriptions* **101**

APPENDIX II *Sample Committee Documents* **105**

APPENDIX III *Sample Grid for Evaluating Board Capital* **111**

APPENDIX IV *Sample Board Meeting Evaluation* **116**

SUGGESTED RESOURCES **119**

ABOUT THE AUTHOR **127**

ABOUT THE BOARDSOURCE GOVERNANCE SERIES

As BoardSource celebrated its 20th anniversary in 2008, we introduced updated editions of the books in the Governance Series, BoardSource's flagship series created to help nonprofit board members understand their primary roles and responsibilities. BoardSource believes that board members and chief executives who know and understand their mutual responsibilities are better equipped to advance their organizations' missions and, in turn, strengthen their communities.

WHY IS A STRONG BOARD IMPORTANT?

There's no denying that the 1.6 million nonprofit organizations in the United States play a vital role in society, from assisting victims of natural disasters to beautifying our neighborhoods, from educating our children to healing the sick. To ensure that their organizations have the resources, leadership, and oversight necessary to carry out these and other vital activities, nonprofit boards must understand and fulfill their governance responsibilities.

Although there have been headline-worthy scandals by a few nonprofits and their boards, the vast majority try hard every day to be worthy of the public's trust. Nevertheless, BoardSource frequently hears from nonprofit board members and chief executives who say that they are not always sure what the basic components of good governance are or how to educate every board member in them so they can serve their organizations and the public in the best possible manner. The revised Governance Series helps bridge this gap in knowledge.

Within the board's broad roles of setting the organization's direction, ensuring necessary resources, and providing oversight, board members wear many hats. They are guardians of the mission; they ensure compliance with legal and financial requirements; and they enforce ethical guidelines for their organization. They are policymakers, fundraisers, ambassadors, partners with the chief executive, and strategic thinkers. They monitor progress, evaluate the performance of the organization and the chief executive, and demonstrate integrity in everything they do on behalf of the organization. Because of their many roles, board members need more than enthusiasm for a cause, passion for a mission, or just "good intentions." They need to understand all of their stewardship responsibilities and perform all of their duties.

WHAT WILL BOARD MEMBERS FIND IN THE BOOKS?

The six books address all of the fundamental elements of service common to most boards, including board member responsibilities, how to structure the board in the most efficient manner, and how to accomplish governance work in the spirit of the mission of the organization.

1. *Ten Basic Responsibilities of Nonprofit Boards, Second Edition* (Book 1) by Richard T. Ingram, describes the 10 core areas of board responsibility.

2. *Legal Responsibilities of Nonprofit Boards, Second Edition* (Book 2) by Bruce R. Hopkins, JD, LLM, elaborates on the board's legal responsibilities, liabilities, and the oversight it should provide to protect the organization.

3. *Financial Responsibilities of Nonprofit Boards, Second Edition* (Book 3) by Andrew S. Lang, CPA, explains board fiduciary responsibilities in the areas of financial oversight and risk management.

4. *Fundraising Responsibilities of Nonprofit Boards, Second Edition* (Book 4) by James M. Greenfield, ACFRE, FAHP, helps board members understand why they should be actively engaged in ensuring adequate resources for the organization — and how to get involved in fundraising.

5. *The Nonprofit Board's Role in Mission, Planning, and Evaluation, Second Edition* (Book 5) by Kay Sprinkel Grace, MA, Amy McClellan, MNO, and John A. Yankey, PhD, shows how to define and communicate the organization's mission and link strategic planning and evaluation to achieve organizational success.

6. *Structures and Practices of Nonprofit Boards, Second Edition* (Book 6) by Charles F. Dambach, MBA, Melissa Davis, and Robert L. Gale offers guidance on how to build and structure the board (size, committees, term limits) and enhance leadership roles and the partnership between the chair and the chief executive.

Each book focuses on one topic, breaking information into manageable amounts that are easy to digest. Readers will find real-world examples that provide insight from effective boards, statistics from the BoardSource *Nonprofit Governance Index 2007* survey of nonprofit organizations, tips and pitfalls, lists of the most important things to remember, end-of-chapter questions, glossaries, and resource lists for further reading. The authors of the books are subject matter experts with years of experience in the nonprofit sector.

WHO SHOULD READ THE BOOKS?

Board members and senior staff, especially chief executives, in nonprofits of all types and sizes will find the information contained in the Governance Series relevant. They can use it to set standards, to develop their own approaches to board work and interacting with board members, and to modify practices as the organization evolves.

There's something in the Governance Series for everyone associated with the board. A board chair, for example, might share Book 5 (*The Nonprofit Board's Role in Mission, Planning, and Evaluation*) with board members before starting a strategic planning process or give Book 4 (*Fundraising Responsibilities of Nonprofit Boards*) to the development committee. Chief executives will find it beneficial to give Book 3 (*Financial Responsibilities of Nonprofit Boards*) to the board treasurer and to review Book 1 (*The Ten Basic Responsibilities of Noprofit Boards*) and give it, along with Book 6 (*Structures and Practices of Nonprofit Boards*), to senior staff and the board chair to clarify board–chief executive roles and strengthen the partnership with the board. All board members will want to read Book 2 (*Legal Responsibilities of Nonprofit Boards*) so they understand how to protect themselves and the organization. The chair of the governance committee might give new board members all six books. This sharing helps ensure that everyone associated with the board is "on the same page" and has a common understanding of the board's responsibilities, expectations, and activities.

Board service entails serious obligations, to be sure, but it can also deliver immense satisfaction. A board that knows what is expected of it and performs at the highest level is a strategic resource for its organization and chief executive. And ultimately, this commitment by dedicated board members translates into mission impact in our communities.

The Governance Series was made possible in part through the support of MetLife Foundation.

INTRODUCTION
ORGANIZED FOR SUCCESS

In days gone by, service on a nonprofit board was often perceived as an honorary role requiring nothing more than periodic attendance at meetings and generous annual donations. Not anymore. Vibrant growth in the nonprofit sector has helped to change the nature of board service. Board members need to do more than just show up. They must understand and promote the organization's work, define measures of success, and assess how well the organization performs using both subjective and objective standards. They must generate and allocate resources, hire the chief executive, develop plans, establish policies and programs, and monitor activities — all with a sharp focus on producing meaningful results.

The way nonprofit boards organize themselves and conduct their affairs determines the value they add to their organizations. To meet the demands of the current nonprofit environment and take full advantage of the opportunities it presents, nonprofit boards must regularly review and revise board structures, practices, and procedures to be sure they have the levels of engagement, flexibility, and responsiveness that will facilitate effective action.

Nonprofit governance may be challenging and demanding, but it is also exciting and rewarding. It calls for

- visionary and vigilant leadership
- efficient and flexible structures
- productive and proven practices
- an inquiring and trusting culture
- a shared passion for the mission

This book provides a set of basic guidelines to enable nonprofit boards to meet these challenges and develop board members who are actively engaged in the life of the organization. It combines and expands upon two earlier volumes from the BoardSource Governance Series to address how the board is organized, who is on the board, and productive ways for board members to work together.

Specifically, Chapter 1 introduces the constructive partnership between board and staff that informs their division of labor, including the board's role in defining and promoting the organization's mission, vision, and values. It also looks at the key activities and processes that boards engage in, from setting policies and building relationships to conducting strategic planning and assessing the organization's activities and performance.

Chapter 2 addresses board composition, from recruiting new members to developing their leadership potential. It also outlines positive approaches to managing board turnover.

Chapter 3 is devoted to the leadership role of the board chair and the relationship between the chair and the chief executive. Chapter 4 explores the structures that facilitate the board's work and includes a brief discussion of basic board committees, task forces, and advisory councils.

Chapter 5 covers all aspects of meetings, with a focus on ensuring productivity. Chapter 6 reflects on the dynamics of the board as a team, while the Conclusion offers a simple yet effective formula for good governance. A group of committed nonprofit leaders contributed to all of these chapters by sharing opinions, examples, practices, and anecdotes, many of which appear throughout the text as well as in informational boxes.

Discussion questions appear at the end of each chapter; these can be used to prompt board dialogue either at regular times set aside on the board meeting agenda or during a board retreat. Appendix I contains sample job descriptions for the chief executive and the board chair. Several sample documents related to committees appear in Appendix II, including a committee charter, an explanation of committee roles, and a form for submitting a committee recommendation for board approval. Appendix III provides a grid that can be used to identify and recruit prospective board members and track recruitment efforts, and Appendix IV offers a sample evaluation form for a board meeting. Finally, an annotated list offers suggested resources for further reading.

Within the United States and throughout the world, governing boards are learning to practice the art of effective governance and restructuring themselves to achieve results. This book will help board members develop, examine, and refine their board's structures and practices so that they can make the best possible use of the time and talents of the remarkable people governing their organization.

CHAPTER 1

THE FOUNDATION OF GOOD GOVERNANCE

Ensuring effective governance of the organization is the most important responsibility facing nonprofit board members and staff today. Understanding what governance is helps board members fulfill their collective responsibility to an organization.

WHAT GOVERNANCE IS

Governance is the activity performed by an entity (such as a board, a city council, or a legislature) that holds authority within a system. In an organizational system such as a nonprofit, authority is granted to the board of directors by the state when the organization is incorporated. The board is authorized to make decisions and set policies that define how the organization will carry out its mission; it is also held accountable for the actions that follow those decisions and policies. The board then governs the organization — that is, it directs and guides the organization from its position of authority.

Governance is group action. Individual board members do not govern the organization; rather, meeting as a group confers governing status to the board as a whole. Governance implies the exercise of power and authority over the organization on behalf of the community it serves.

MISSION, VISION, AND VALUES

To meet the challenges of the nonprofit environment, boards need members who understand governance as a dynamic activity. They need board members who are fully and actively engaged in promoting the organization's achievement of its mission, developing and refining its vision, and upholding its values. The first order of business for board members is to understand and endorse these defining elements of the organization's identity.

MISSION AND MISSION STATEMENT

Everything begins with the mission. Despite the emergence of new leadership models, the mission remains the foremost organizing tool for a nonprofit, helping to build common understanding and ensuring that programs and activities are aligned toward the same goal.

The board's role is to define, refine, and advance the mission of the nonprofit organization it governs, and the primary purpose of every board meeting is to make governance decisions that will help the organization fulfill its mission. Every board vote on every proposal should take into account the effect of the decision on the organization's ability to achieve its mission.

The mission is readily kept in mind — by both board members and staff — when it is formulated in a mission statement. An effective mission statement is clear, concise, and compelling. It explains in a few words why the organization exists. It serves as the guideline by which all governance and management decisions are made.

Board members who can express their organization's mission quickly, clearly, and confidently have taken the first step toward working collaboratively to achieve it. They also are able to focus on outcomes. These boards recognize the fundamental link between reports on results and outcomes and a consistent focus on the mission. They continually seek more comprehensive ways to measure results in terms of mission achievement.

VISION AND VISION STATEMENT

Mission statements alone do not provide all of the guidance the board needs to govern. The organization also needs to articulate a vision statement and a set of values. While the mission statement explains why the organization exists, the vision statement lays out where it is going. The vision statement conveys the ideal that the organization strives to make real by pursuing its mission; it sets the organization's sights toward the end result for mission accomplishment. In this sense, the mission is the motivator for the vision.

RELATIONSHIP BETWEEN VISION STATEMENTS AND MISSION STATEMENTS

ORGANIZATION TYPE	VISION STATEMENT	MISSION STATEMENT
COMMUNITY ART MUSEUM	A community in which the visual arts are valued, promoted, and preserved as expressions of human creativity and representatives of common human experience	To stimulate community-wide appreciation of and commitment to the visual arts and their creators
NEIGHBORHOOD CLINIC	A city in which all citizens have access to the health care they need and the knowledge, motivation, and resources to adopt and maintain healthy lifestyles	To contribute to a healthy citizenry by providing services, education, access, and motivation for all
LITERACY COUNCIL	A county in which all citizens have the language skills they need to achieve work and life goals, and none are disenfranchised, unemployed, or underemployed because they lack fundamental communication (literacy and oracy) skills	To outfit everyone in the county to realize their personal and professional goals by ensuring appropriate literacy education

The vision statement is by nature visionary — that is, it is likely to articulate a dream that will never be fully realized. Nevertheless, every nonprofit organization should have a vision statement as well as a mission statement. The vision statement provides the inspiration, and the mission statement the motivation, to serve the community in specific ways. Together, the vision and the mission form a call to action that not only informs the public about the organization's reason for existence but also encourages people to become part of it.

Both the board and the chief executive must be integrally involved in developing the organization's mission statement and vision statement and must schedule regular review of them to ensure that they remain current. The chief executive should also involve the rest of the staff in the development phase because participation is the most effective way to get the buy-in from the staff that ultimately will do the bulk of the work of carrying out this mission.

Without a shared understanding of — and passion for — the mission and vision of the organization, the board and chief executive will not be able to purposefully set, accomplish, or oversee organizational goals. By collaborating with the staff on development and review of these statements and giving staff input serious consideration, the board can ensure that the vision statement and mission statement represent the organization accurately and fully and that all are committed to them.

VALUES

Values are the principles and ideals that govern the way the organization conducts its affairs. They define the cultural norms that should inform the behavior of board and staff. Board members and staff articulate core organizational values and use them to guide their behavior and decisions.

The organization should describe these core values in writing. Doing so defines the organization's standard of behavior and emphasizes that one standard applies to everyone, whether board or staff; to every decision that is made; and to every activity. Many organizations espouse core values such as honesty, responsibility, integrity, transparency, compassion, and mutual respect — but it is counterproductive to borrow someone else's values. Each organization needs to identify its own set of cultural norms and inspiration.

VALUES IN ACTION

YMCA volunteers and staff in the United States filter decisions and actions through a set of shared values by asking: Is this decision (action, choice, program, request, response, brochure) caring? Is it honest? Is it responsible? Does it show respect? These are the core values of YMCA of the USA, of Canada, and of other national movements; some add an additional value or two.

If the answer is not "yes" to all four questions, the asker goes back to the drawing board. If the answers are all "yes," then the designer uses values to devise the implementation steps.

In this case, caring, respect, and honesty would guide the selection of words to convey the decision; respect would determine who should receive information about the decision; and responsibility and honesty would infuse every step of the action.

Articulating the organization's values in writing contributes to the effective functioning of the board. The organization's values define a standard of conduct for board member collaboration and interaction with staff. They also provide guidance that enables the board to establish policies that are fair and balanced and to know what it is assessing — and why — when conducting organizational evaluation. Organizations are well-served when boards take time to confront and resolve questions of value and adopt policies accordingly.

For more information on mission, vision, and values, see *The Nonprofit Board's Role in Mission, Planning, and Evaluation*, Book 5 in the BoardSource Governance Series.

A CONSTRUCTIVE PARTNERSHIP: BOARD AND STAFF

In addition to agreeing on the mission, vision, and values, board members and staff need a shared understanding of the different roles they play in the organization. The days of nonprofits run by well-meaning but untrained people willing to work for little or no pay, dependent on the board for management support and program implementation, have ended. Nonprofit management has become a career choice, and professional staff, with their special training and years of experience, expect to be respected and paid as professionals — because they are.

The relationship between board and staff has also evolved, from board control and staff submission to constructive partnership. While the board recognizes that it supervises and evaluates the chief executive, board members appreciate that forging a mutually supportive partnership will render the whole greater than the sum of the parts. The partnership is sustained when board members and staff members respect and trust one another, communicate openly and honestly, and know that everyone at the table is motivated by the well-being of the organization.

TIP

Although the chief executive should always be viewed as the primary link between board and staff, the organization can clearly benefit from open lines of communication and interaction among board members and key staff. This is especially true if the board has committees whose oversight roles dovetail with specific staff responsibilities, such as finance, program, and fundraising. One caveat: Board members and board committees should channel any requests of the staff through the chief executive. This allows the chief executive to make sure staff time is not being squandered on redundant or unnecessary tasks.

Successful nonprofit leadership requires that an organization's board and staff understand and commit to fulfilling their respective roles. They recognize a division of labor, defining which responsibilities are shared and which are specific to board chair, board members, chief executive, and staff. As an example, many chief executives help the board formulate policy. Although the board determines policy guidelines, the chief executive implements policy decisions, and the board — with the help of staff — monitors the results.

The exact way in which roles and responsibilities are divided and shared, however, differs from one organization to another. In larger and more established organizations that have a significant level of staffing, boards do not become involved in day-to-day details. New organizations and those with smaller staffs, by contrast, may rely to some degree on board members to assist with budgeting, legal matters, and other areas where the staff lacks expertise.

The board chair and the chief executive should take the lead in helping board and staff members define their respective responsibilities. In general, the staff should have responsibility for operations and program implementation; the board should devote its time to oversight and strategic issues. In addition, because most committee work involves both board and staff members, the chief executive and the board chair should establish board–staff communication guidelines so that everyone knows how to communicate without undermining the authority of the chief executive. The overall goal should be to maintain an atmosphere of collegiality and mutual respect.

BOARD PRACTICES: OVERSIGHT, RESOURCES, AND PLANNING

The major role of the board is to ensure the ongoing viability of the organization. To fulfill this responsibility, effective boards engage in three types of practices:

- They provide oversight to ensure that the organization is financially healthy, maintains focus on its vision, fulfills its mission, and acts in accordance with its values.

- They make certain that the organization has the resources necessary to continue its work and to grow.

- They identify the broad directions for development that will support and enhance the organization's ability to fulfill its mission.

PROVIDING OVERSIGHT

Board oversight of a nonprofit organization should not be confused with management. Oversight involves looking at the big picture and relating current projects, outcomes, and ways of operating to the achievement of the organization's mission. The board's oversight role includes the following activities.

Monitoring the Organization's Finances. The board provides financial oversight to the organization by regularly reviewing its financial status. The board's finance committee is charged with regular examination of the organization's financial statements, but the board as a whole should review actual income and expenses against the budget at least quarterly. Such a review is part of each board member's fiduciary responsibility to the organization. The review should include opportunities for all board members to ask questions and satisfy themselves that they are fully informed about the organization's financial situation.

One important financial oversight mechanism for a nonprofit board is an independent audit. An outside auditor examines the organization's fiscal policies and procedures, comparing them with generally accepted accounting principles (GAAP) to determine whether the organization's accounting is objective, complete, and reflects reality. An independent audit can help assure the board — and the public — that the organization has sufficient accountability and control mechanisms in place.

Boards also have an obligation to the community to make certain that their organizations' operations advance the purposes that initially qualified them to be tax exempt. To fulfill this obligation, boards must ensure that staff members follow processes to submit the organization's annual Form 990 (or 990-PF) to the IRS and make it available to the public. Many nonprofit organizations distribute printed annual reports to stakeholders, donors, elected officials, members of the media, and members of the community, in addition to publicly posting the same financial information and programmatic achievements on their Web sites.

For more information on oversight, see *Financial Responsibilities of Nonprofit Boards,* Book 3 in the BoardSource Governance Series.

PITFALL

A board should guard against balancing the budget by "borrowing" from the physical assets (for example, by deferring routine annual maintenance) or from the human assets (for example, by providing salaries and benefits that are below what is appropriate). Such a short-term action can have negative consequences in the long term.

Setting Policies. A nonprofit board assumes responsibility for the organization's compliance with legal and ethical obligations. To ensure legal compliance, transparency, and accountability — and alignment of activities with the organization's stated values — the board formulates policies and procedures to guide its work and the work of the organization. The board may need to develop policies specific to the organization and its circumstances, but several types of policies apply to all nonprofits.

- *Conflict-of-Interest Policy.* The duty of loyalty that a member accepts when joining a nonprofit board guarantees that the best interests of the organization will prevail over any private interest of the member, the member's family, or the member's employer. In addition, any information to which a board member is privy will be used in the best interest of the organization. Establishing and enforcing a conflict-of-interest policy that supports this duty helps protect the organization from unethical and illegal practices and demonstrates that its practices align with its stated purpose of serving the public interest.

  Boards ask members to complete a conflict-of-interest disclosure form when they join the board and once a year during their terms. On the form, board members disclose all matters or interests in which they are engaged that involve (or appear to involve) the nonprofit. New board members should be educated on how to recognize a conflict (or the appearance of a conflict) and the procedures to follow when a conflict becomes apparent.

Besides explaining what constitutes a conflict of interest and who is implicated, the policy should outline the board's process of dealing with the conflict. This process, at a minimum, should highlight disclosure and recusal. Often, it also includes the expectation for the board member in question to leave the room for the discussion and voting and, in extreme situations, to resign. Ultimately, the policy should also clarify the consequences for violating the policy, which may include dismissal.

- *Whistleblower and Document-Retention Policies.* Two provisions in the Sarbanes-Oxley Act of 2002 require nonprofit compliance. First, no organization can retaliate against an employee who reports suspected illegal or unethical practices. Second, no organization may modify, discard, or destroy its documents while an investigation of such an allegation is underway.

To ensure compliance with these two provisions and answer "yes" to the IRS on Form 990's question about whether the organization has specific policies, the board may wish to develop a whistleblower policy and outline the procedures to follow when making or receiving a report. The board may also develop a document-retention policy to protect the organization's important documents and records, including those related to state and federal tax-exemption, board minutes, and policies and to ensure no destruction of documents takes place before or during a federal investigation.

For more information on conflict-of-interest and whistleblower policies, see *Legal Responsibilities of Nonprofit Boards,* Book 2 in the BoardSource Governance Series.

PITFALL

Before the board discusses a major financial transaction or other issue where contact with the constituents may arise, it makes sense for the chair to review the conflict-of-interest disclosure forms on file. However, simply relying on these forms to detect the presence of a conflict of interest is not enough. Many conflicts are case specific — they are not evident a year ahead of time or could not have been anticipated prior to the meeting. To avoid perfunctory review and signature, add real examples and issues when distributing disclosure forms to board members. Emphasize the importance of the disclosures by asking members to assess their own situations before each discussion.

Monitoring and Evaluating Progress in Achieving Mission. To fulfill its obligation to the public, a board must hold itself accountable for what happens in the organization by regularly measuring the effectiveness and impact of the organization's activities. A comprehensive process includes both performance and program evaluations.

The board should frame evaluation as a constructive process that assesses a task, individual, work group, process, skill, behavior, or attitude in order to identify strengths and suggest ways of improving. The board should clearly support the implementation of any changes.

- *Assessing the Board.* Evaluation of the board's work in a culture of trust and high expectation must happen continuously. An assessment is not a report card; it is a developmental tool. Boards that intentionally schedule routine checkups will spot ways to strengthen their performance.

A formal assessment examines the board's performance in all areas of its responsibilities. It gauges how well the board has served the organization and, equally important, how the board could improve. Formal assessments, typically undertaken every few years, may include evaluations of the board's collective productivity and individual members' contributions, plus guided reflections during a multiday retreat on how to improve structures and practices. They should examine the composition of the board, its capacity to identify and recruit new members, its relationship with its constituents and the chief executive, the appropriateness of the committee structure, and the effectiveness of board meetings.

Boards often engage an external consultant to facilitate the formal assessment process. An outside facilitator trained and experienced in self-assessment techniques can guide the organization through the sensitive process with minimal internal anxiety. This reinforces the anonymity of responses and encourages candor. An objective outside expert also brings a wider perspective on the board's performance along with fresh approaches to suggest.

A full-scale formal assessment isn't needed every year. Between formal retreat-based assessments, boards can quickly and effectively evaluate their performance with mini self-assessments that take a few minutes to complete, possibly during board meetings. To ensure anonymity, the governance committee — the standing committee charged with ensuring the board's long-term development — collects the forms and tabulates and presents the results on the spot, without attribution or accusation. Based on its review and discussion of the results, the larger group will know whether board members share similar perceptions of the board's performance and can identify areas that need strengthening.

WHAT ASSESSMENT CAN ACHIEVE

In *The Board Building Cycle, Second Edition* (BoardSource, 2007, Berit M. Lakey outlines these functions and outcomes of the board self-assessment process.

Functions

- Measure the board's progress
- Identify areas that need improving
- Establish goals for the future
- Remind members of their responsibilities
- Help reshape the board's operations
- Build trust
- Facilitate communication among members and the chief executive

Common outcomes

- Strategic planning initiatives
- Improvements in monitoring program effectiveness
- Enhanced board meetings and a more effective use of committees
- Improvements in the process for reviewing the chief executive's performance
- Strategies for more intentional board recruitment
- Establishment of a governance committee and of a more thoughtful nomination process

- *Assessing the Chief Executive.* Normally, the chief executive is the only staff member assessed by the board. (In many performing arts organizations, both the artistic director and the managing director report to the board and have their performance evaluated by the board.) The chief executive is responsible for aligning the work of the entire staff with the organization's goals and answers for the organization's ability to meet them.

As part of its succession planning (see Chapter 3), the board should develop an annual chief executive evaluation process that clearly articulates roles for the board chair, other board members, and possibly staff. The board chair might name a few board members (or work with the executive committee) to conduct the evaluation, which compares the chief executive's actual performance against annual goals agreed upon the previous year. The process may include gathering feedback from other board members or even from staff, if the chief executive has agreed to it. The chair and the assessment team share the evaluation's results with the full board during an executive session to obtain agreement with the final report.

Timing the evaluation to coincide with the end of the fiscal year provides results upon which to substantiate the assessment and allows the chief executive to set new goals that align with the organization's goals for the coming year. These goals, which serve as the basis for the following year's evaluation, are mutually agreed upon by the chief executive and the board over the course of several discussions.

THE ANNUAL APPRAISAL

BoardSource's *Nonprofit Governance Index 2007* indicates that 74 percent of the boards responding had evaluated the chief executive formally. Surprisingly, only 74 percent of those shared the results with the full board!

- *Assessing the Organization.* To fulfill its commitment to the organization's stated purpose, the nonprofit board uses a variety of measures to monitor and assess the organization's performance, efficiency, and impact. Because it allocates resources and sets goals, the board must evaluate whether resources are used effectively, meet the goals to which they were attached, and advance the mission.

  Organizational assessment requires an active partnership between staff and board, with each contributing different yet equally valuable perspectives. Drawing upon output and outcome data, personal experiences, external feedback, benchmarks against peers, and financial metrics — including calculating a qualitative and quantitative return on investment — the board monitors progress toward accomplishment of the strategic plan and assesses the quality of service delivery.

To facilitate routine monitoring, the board and the chief executive need to agree on critical indicators and efficient methods of reviewing them. Some major indicators are internal, relating the organization's performance to its mission, vision, and priorities. Others are external, relating the organization's performance to that of comparable organizations, to the needs of the community, and to the operating environment.

The board also monitors programmatic activities and outcomes in the light of environmental and industry conditions and trends. To ensure that the organization's goals and operations remain current and relevant, the board may make midcourse corrections and revisit strategic and operating plans. Together with the chief executive, boards depend on assessment data as well as telltale signs when considering the introduction, continuation, or cessation of programs.

For more information on organizational assessment, see *The Nonprofit Board's Role in Mission, Planning, and Evaluation*, Book 5 in the BoardSource Governance Series.

PRINCIPLES OF SOUND PRACTICE

In 2007, the Panel on the Nonprofit Sector, convened by the Independent Sector, developed and published 33 sector-wide principles to promote self-regulation of nonprofit organizations. *Principles for Good Governance and Ethical Practice: A Guide for Charities and Foundations* offers guidance to boards in four categories:

- legal compliance and public disclosure

- effective governance

- strong financial oversight

- responsible fundraising

These are available at www.independentsector.org.

Ensuring Adequate Resources

When recruiting, boards frequently emphasize the role of board members in securing the financial resources to deliver programs and services consistent with the organization's mission and promise, as well as to attract and retain highly qualified and motivated staff. That partially translates into engaging in fundraising activities as a donor and door opener. The larger responsibility includes ascertaining the best mix of, and most promising strategies for securing, resources — individual and foundation contributions, membership dues, fee-bearing programs, annual and capital campaigns, endowment development, for-profit ventures — from which to guarantee the organization's future.

While having the potential to strengthen many organizations, some projects carry the risk of diverting the board's attention from the central mission. Boards must determine the wisdom and viability of financial ventures, creating policies and budgets that balance the opportunities to generate earned income with programs and services that genuinely advance the mission.

In addition to ensuring that the organization has adequate financial resources, a board is responsible for two other categories of resources:

Human Resources. While the board oversees only the chief executive, it ensures the financial resources for securing top talent in a competitive arena and insists upon training, development, and evaluation systems for all staff.

Public Credibility. Maintaining a positive public image influences all other resources. Board members are partners in communicating the organization's progress on mission to external audiences, supporting a dynamic communication plan, and delivering key messages to assigned constituencies. In addition, members must take personal responsibility to reflect the mission in their own public and personal lives.

Engaging in Planning

Whether envisioning the organization's long-term future or approving next year's budget, board members need to approach their work with a deliberate mind-set. Every issue they consider, every decision they make, should involve thinking strategically — asking "what if" questions and spinning out "suppose this happens" scenarios. With a strategic culture always in place and evident at every meeting, a board, in concert with the chief executive, can easily apply that thinking to the formal planning activities it engages in periodically.

Strategic Planning. Development of a strategic plan to guide the organization's future is based on strategic thinking. Drawing on quantitative data and informed opinion about both the internal dynamic of the organization and external factors that affect it, the board reaffirms the mission and engages in a formal process of determining the actions that can move the organization forward over two to three years.

The outcome is a strategic plan that

- positions the organization for ongoing success by consciously building on organizational strengths while addressing areas of weakness

- articulates priorities and directions

- lays out measurable goals with action steps for goal accomplishment

- guides the committee and task force structure that the board adopts in order to address the plan's objectives

- provides a guide for decision making; the plan comes alive through operational plans that flow from the strategies

- influences board agendas to allocate the lion's share of meeting time to discussion of progress toward goals

- translates priorities into action plans for board members, identifying specific ways that the board and its members can contribute to the organization's success

- provides a framework for the work of the chief executive and the staff and a means for the board to monitor and evaluate progress against goals

- serves as a basis for assessing the chief executive and the board's own performance in pursuit of mission

Finally, the plan lays the groundwork for shaping board recruitment and fine-tuning future planning. For more information on strategic planning, see *The Nonprofit Board's Role in Mission, Planning, and Evaluation,* Book 5 in the BoardSource Governance Series.

FORMULATING A PLAN

Mindy R. Wertheimer outlines these basic steps in strategic planning in *The Board Chair Handbook, Second Edition* (BoardSource, 2007):

- Develop or reaffirm mission statement.

- Conduct an internal organizational assessment.

- Conduct an environmental scan.

- Examine strategic issues.

- Formulate strategic goals and priorities.

- Create action plans.

- Monitor and evaluate implementation of the strategic plan.

Protective Planning. As stewards of the organization's assets, boards regularly ask management to review and report on current and potential risks to the organization. Sometimes that means designating a committee — in many cases, the audit committee — to review programmatic and operational risk issues. Once risks are identified, the board establishes procedures for managing them, such as

- providing appropriate and sufficient insurance for board members, staff, programmatic and operational activities, and property

- developing contingency plans, including emergency preparedness plans for natural or other disasters

- recognizing and addressing risks to the organization's standing with the general public

Margaret L. Ackerley provides an example in "Legal. Ethical. Exceptional." (*Board Member*®, January/February 2006), noting that the board of The Nature Conservancy established a Conservation Projects and Practices subcommittee commissioned "to review activities that are of 'first instance' or that present reputational risk to the organization." The subcommittee enables the board to protect the organization by identifying risks to the organization's public image and bringing them to the attention of the full board.

Succession Planning. Recognizing that good governance begins with people who can do the most to fulfill the mission, effective organizations take a strategic approach to developing future leaders. They develop a transparent and participatory succession planning process that assesses future organizational needs and the competencies and interests of current board members and staff. Then they intentionally plan for leadership transition by grooming potential committee chairs, task force leaders, and board officers — as well as potential successors to the chief executive (see Chapter 3).

QUESTIONS THE BOARD SHOULD ASK

1. Do we periodically revisit our mission statement to ensure it is clear, concise, and compelling?

2. Does everyone on the board and staff understand our mission? Are we all committed to it?

3. How do we test policy, program, and budget decisions to ensure they are congruent with the mission and in alignment with vision and values?

4. What evidence (actions, discussions, educational events, etc.) can we cite from the last year to prove that the organization is fulfilling its mission?

5. How does our organization demonstrate transparency in its activities? How does our organization demonstrate accountability to the public?

6. How would we handle and address a conflict of interest that arose in a board meeting?

7. What process do we have in place to evaluate the chief executive?

8. Do our strategic plan, agendas, and minutes verify that we allocate the majority of our time to determining the organization's future?

9. How would we handle and address any allegations of wrongdoing within the organization?

2

CHAPTER 2

BUILDING A BOARD

There is no fixed formula for determining the size and composition of a board. Form follows function. The ability of a nonprofit board to help an organization reach its goals depends entirely on how decisions are made and by whom, so each organization needs to evaluate its own needs and priorities and build its board accordingly.

SIZE

According to BoardSource's *Nonprofit Governance Index 2007,* the average board has 16 members. By no means does this number represent the optimal size for every board. The best size for any given organization is what the board determines it should be after assessing organizational needs and what is necessary to accomplish them. If the board agrees to adjust the size, it must amend its bylaws to reflect the change.

Not every board has the opportunity to determine its own size. In many formal membership organizations, external factors influence the board's size. For example, special mandates may require that a certain number of board seats be reserved for various constituencies or geographic regions. Or, outside authorities may have the opportunity to nominate board members to represent their specific interests. Some of these boards may be rather large in size and need to figure out their own solutions to deal with accompanying challenges.

One rationale for larger boards is rooted in the notion that more is better. According to this rationale, a larger board can provide both broader representation of the organization's constituency and a larger base of donors and fundraisers. The more people you have with whom to share the workload, the less burnout and stress individual board members experience. Furthermore, with a larger board, more people who want to serve have the opportunity — even if willingness to join the board does not necessarily bring with it the needed expertise and perspectives that the board seeks.

Larger boards, however, are not necessarily more effective or productive. The more members who are available to contribute ideas and opinions, the longer consensus building tends to take — and the more slowly the board may move from discussion to action. In addition, large boards tend to leave many members feeling underutilized and unappreciated. On large boards, members may have few opportunities to speak at meetings; because their votes are diluted by so many other votes, they may not feel their participation matters or that their time has been valued. The chair has the responsibility to determine when the issue has been handled thoroughly with all the sides having been presented fairly.

PITFALL

If all members of a 30-member board are actively engaged in debate and want to comment on an issue, it would take a full hour for each to speak for just two minutes. With such a large board, either the meetings have to be very long or some members will be unable to share their opinions.

Smaller groups tend to expedite communication. The smaller the board, the more important each individual member is to the organization, the more is expected of each member — and the more each can contribute to policy discussions. With smaller boards, members can communicate more personally and achieve consensus more easily, facilitating the move from discussion to action.

If the board is too small, however, it may lack the people needed to carry out all board tasks effectively. The board's outreach capability — so essential for building community relations, raising funds, and recruiting new board members — will diminish as the number of active board members decreases.

Furthermore, the lower the number of active bo[...]
the greater the risk of board member burnout.

Each organization needs to look at its mission and the m[...]
that it will carry out in pursuit of that mission, then determine
how large a board it needs to operate effectively. That is, the
board needs to be purposefully constructed; it must strike a
balance in which each member feels valued and appreciated,
no member feels overburdened, and all board functions can be
fully carried out.

COMPOSITION

Like its size, the board's composition should be addressed
intentionally and strategically so that its members provide the
best possible leadership for the organization. Identification and
recruitment of new board members should take into account the
specific skills, expertise, and resources that the organization
needs (see Appendix III).

In addition, and perhaps more important, it should consider
diversity and personal attributes or characteristics. Associations
and federated organizations, for example, might consider
including at-large board members if the board otherwise is
composed of regional or chapter representatives. These
"unattached" members tend to bring additional balance to
perspectives and allow the board to focus on potentially
missing qualities or skills that otherwise might go ignored.

Expertise and Resources. Board member prospecting and
recruiting needs to identify people with the capacity to provide
the strategic vision, guidance, resources, and oversight that the
organization requires. The search for new board members begins
with an examination of the resources the board will need to
meet organizational goals during the next few years. The
strategic plan, accompanied by the organization's mission and its
stage of development, guides the prospecting process.

For example, a start-up community theater will have very
different requirements from the board of a regional theater with
a 50-year track record. The fledgling organization will need
board members who are qualified and prepared to supplement

the work of the two-person staff, while the established theater will face major fundraising responsibilities to offset expansion of seats and the season.

Diversity. Boards need to reflect the diversity of the community that the organization serves and takes advantage of the dynamic interaction that accompanies such diversity. Shifts toward greater racial, ethnic, linguistic, and religious diversity; toward young people outnumbering older adults in some parts of the country; and toward more women in roles and sectors previously dominated by men have prompted nonprofit organizations to rethink the traditional make-up of their boards. People with wide-ranging experiences and perspectives contribute new and creative ideas that expand a board's intellectual capacity.

And it turns out that diverse groups are more productive than homogeneous groups. In *The Difference: How the Power of Diversity Creates Better Groups, Firms, Schools and Societies* (Princeton University Press, 2007), Scott Page contends that diverse groups bring more "tools" to the table. Those tools result from different ways of looking at, getting stuck on, and solving problems.

According to Page, homogeneous groups with similar educations, backgrounds, addresses, and affiliations tend to think and get stuck in the same way. The more diverse the members of a group tackling a problem are, the more likely they are to quickly generate multiple solutions. If they get stuck, they get stuck in different places! Boards without redundancy may be better prepared to steer organizations effectively and efficiently through the complex nonprofit environment.

PITFALL

When the board chair, chief executive, and governance committee build a board of clones who say "yes" to everything, the resulting group think can mean the organization misses out on opportunities to try something new. A truly dynamic board benefits from a variety of vigorous leaders.

Personal Attributes. In many ways, the personal attributes of potential board members are more important than their professional expertise. Commitment to the organization, energy to develop initiatives and see them through to completion, and motivation to serve the community are key characteristics of strong board members. An organization cannot purchase these characteristics like it can professional expertise and services.

Positive personal attributes, important within the boardroom, become crucial outside of it. Individual board members perform multiple tasks on behalf of the board. In the community, they serve as ambassadors and advocates, as door-openers and connectors; they also share personal assets for the good of the organization. The stronger their enthusiasm for the organization and the greater their excitement about its mission, the better able they will be to fulfill these roles.

 TIP

When recruiting new board members, don't shy away from approaching community and business leaders you assume won't have the interest or the time to serve. You never know who will be interested in the mission of your organization — and there is nothing like a big-name board member to raise your organization's profile and open doors to new opportunities for funding, partnerships, and more. In most cases, the organization will need to cultivate the prospective board member before the ask, just as it would cultivate a potential major donor.

CULTIVATION AND RECRUITMENT

The board usually delegates the identification and cultivation of potential board members to its governance committee, even though all board members should keep their eyes and ears open for potential candidates. The governance committee intentionally taps and appraises relationships to gauge the best fit. It surveys former board members as well as the board chair, the chief executive, and all board members. Assigning promising prospects to committees, task forces, or other volunteer activities provides each party with a mutual tryout.

While the cultivation process does not guarantee board membership, it narrows the choice of candidates. That way, when the board is ready to bring on a new member, the governance committee is prepared to nominate someone. When nomination time arrives, the governance committee ensures, through research and interviews, that those who meet the standards and show the most promise are willing to serve if nominated and elected.

PITFALL

Prematurely offering a board seat to a prospect, without following appropriate cultivation steps, may produce a "letterhead" board member who isn't ready or willing to devote the necessary time and attention to your organization.

While the governance committee manages the cultivation process, recruitment itself is a team effort. Many organizations invite prospective members to a social event so they can meet current board members. Such an event allows both sides to assess the fit and obtain answers to any remaining questions. All current board members should attend such events so that the prospects gain a complete picture of the group they will be joining and the board as a whole can express its interest in the prospects.

An essential task for the governance committee is ensuring that prospective board members understand the commitment they will be making if elected. Every board member agrees to be held to three legal standards against which actions will be appraised: the duty of care, the duty of loyalty, and the duty of obedience. The governance committee is responsible for making sure that prospective board members recognize and accept this legal obligation.

THREE LEGAL STANDARDS

All actions taken by a board are held to three legal standards. These collective duties, which apply to the entire board, require the active participation of all individual board members. If ever the board or individual board members are sued, their actions or nonactions are judged against these legal obligations. The three Ds, as these standards are often called, set the basic guidelines for the board to act as the fiduciary and the steward of the organization.

Duty of Care. Standard of care in decision making that can be expected of all prudent individuals under similar circumstances. Each board member is to act in good faith and actively participate in governance by

- attending and coming prepared to meetings of the board and appropriate committees

- asking probing questions and using independent judgment

- frequently reviewing the organization's finances and financial policies

Duty of Loyalty. A standard of faithfulness to the organization's priorities. Board members put the interests of the organization ahead of their own professional or personal interests or those of another. This duty is carried out by

- disclosing any conflicts of interest

- adhering to the organization's conflict-of-interest policy

- avoiding the use of corporate opportunities for individual personal gain

- not disclosing confidential information about the organization

Duty of Obedience. A standard of faithfulness to the organization's mission and purpose, which requires that nonprofit directors comply with applicable federal, state, and local laws; adhere to the organization's bylaws; and remain the guardians of the mission. This duty is carried out by

- making decisions that fall within the scope of the organization's mission and governing documents

- complying with all regulatory and reporting requirements, such as filing IRS Form 990 and paying employment taxes

- examining all documents governing the organization and its operation, such as the bylaws, and ensuring they are up-to-date and followed

ELECTION

The organization's bylaws should define the process and procedures for selecting its board. In self-perpetuating boards, the board is responsible for rejuvenating itself. In formal membership organizations, the members usually have the right to elect the board and maybe even the officers. Some boards may have members nominated by external bodies that have a vested interest in the internal affairs of the organization.

Whoever ultimately votes on the board members, it makes sense to engage the governance committee in the process to educate everyone involved on what the board needs and who the potential candidates are.

ORIENTATION

The orientation process actually begins during the cultivation stages. The introductory discussion explains the basic purpose, goals, programs, and services of the organization. Later, when the person becomes a board prospect, a member of the governance committee describes the organization's expectations of a board member, including time commitments and other contributions. Such clarifications help ensure a proper fit between the organization and the prospect before the latter is invited to stand for election.

Once new members are elected, the governance committee oversees a thorough orientation to the organization, to the board, and to roles and responsibilities. Without an orientation, board members may never achieve their potential as contributing members of the team. Each member deserves a multilayered orientation that includes a formal group session supported by a board manual, potentially a tour of program sites, introductions to key staff, a knowledgeable mentor, and a personal conversation with the board chair and chief executive.

The formal orientation goes beyond a review of important written documents, board structure, and meeting schedules. It should connect the new member to the organization, its history, and the accomplishments and the aspirations of the board. Other board members — past and present — and their selected stories are more conducive to building commitment to mission than are flowcharts and travel reimbursement forms.

Incorporating interactive training and dialogue into orientation enables everyone to become better acquainted with each new board member's needs, interests, experiences, and expertise. Discussions, case studies, and role-playing help new board members understand their responsibilities and demonstrate what they bring to the organization. By establishing rapport between new and continuing board members, this training lays the foundation for the ongoing open communication that enables the board to function effectively as a group.

Orientation encompasses more than an information session or two. New members have needs and aspirations that led them to accept the role, and fulfilling those takes a sustained effort by the governance committee and board leaders. For instance, to facilitate each new member's development during the first year, leaders might

- advocate appropriate committee assignments to new members to best utilize their talents

- assign a veteran board member as a mentor. Offering such support, at least through the first year, readies new members for service sooner and imbues them with greater confidence.

- provide motivation in the form of responsibilities. One organization drafts new members to serve as greeters at each board meeting so they become better connected and more confident early in their terms.

- conduct a "reality check" halfway through the first year of service. A breakfast for new members, for example, might include a question-and-answer session and serve as an informal means of assessing their future leadership potential.

PITFALL

Loading the orientation with housekeeping items — such as how to book your hotel or submit a reimbursement form — leaves little time for building the relationship with the mission, the organization's aspirations, and other board members.

TERM LIMITS AND RE-ELECTION

Boards benefit from fresh perspectives, stagnate from the status quo, and deteriorate when closed groups predominate. Many boards revitalize themselves by adopting term limits that specify the number of years that a board member can serve continuously. Others do not limit the number of times a member can be re-elected. Whatever approach is used, the governance committee needs to candidly and thoroughly evaluate each member's performance and move unproductive members off the board.

Term limits offer the advantage of regular turnover. They also offer a graceful exit point for board members who are often absent, ineffective, or simply overwhelmed by other responsibilities. The organizations that responded to BoardSource's *Nonprofit Governance Index 2007* report an average board term of 3.1 years, with board members eligible to serve an average of 2.3 consecutive terms. When adopted, term limits should stagger the terms of individual board members so that all current members will not retire from the board in any given year.

TIP

When introducing staggered term limits to a board, start by asking for volunteers to be assigned to various groups. Some board members, for example, may be ready to conclude their service to the board as soon as the new system begins. That way, you do not have to arbitrarily determine who leaves the board immediately and who stays for an extra few years.

Term limits have the disadvantage of causing the board to lose members with hard-to-replace expertise, institutional memory, or other helpful resources. To guard against such losses, boards should ensure that others are developing the skills and knowledge necessary to take on the roles vacated by departing members. Boards should also make an effort to retain retiring members' support or influence, perhaps by asking them to join a committee, task force, or advisory council.

Exit interviews conducted by the governance committee may identify such alternative connections to the organization beyond board service. Former board members who are still passionate about the organization and its mission are assets. Disgruntled ones are liabilities.

Whether or not an organization imposes term limits, board members should not view re-election to the board as a sure thing. The governance committee is responsible for rigorously evaluating board member performance before extending any member's term. It should carefully and confidentially evaluate members who are eligible for re-election in terms of the needs of the board and of the members' past performance and interest in serving another term. If the organization's priorities call for someone with different qualifications, for instance, the governance committee should recommend against renominating a current member in favor of bringing in someone with the identified prerequisites.

Rarely, if ever, will a board achieve the perfect mix and balance of characteristics and skills. Nevertheless, incorporating effective structures and practices into board work equips leaders to steer the direction of the organization consistent with its mission, vision, and values. Every board should seriously analyze its needs, define the ideal board, then strive to achieve it.

Assessment is recommended when a member reaches the end of a term and is eligible for re-election. The governance committee asks each incumbent eligible for another term to complete a self-evaluation well in advance of the board election. The self-evaluation, followed by a conversation with the board chair,

- helps incumbents consider whether they are interested in re-election

- reminds them of their responsibilities if re-elected

- encourages them to estimate their value and fit in light of their past performance

- provides the governance committee with information that allows it to determine whether to recommend re-nomination

PITFALL

If board members interpret a self-assessment as a request for readiness to serve another term, they may treat it as perfunctory and respond that they are happy to continue on the board. The more specific to the organization's plans and the environmental challenges the questions are, the more likely members will provide thoughtful answers and prepare for the possibility of not serving another term.

While self-assessment has clear relevance when a board member's term is ending, many boards ask all members to assess their performance and set personal goals annually. By asking each board member to reflect in writing on contributions made and successes achieved, aspects of board service that have been especially rewarding, and goals for future activity, the governance committee can help members gain insight into the effects of their actions on the well-being of the organization and identify new ways to contribute.

In addition, particularly if followed by a conversation with the board chair or the governance committee chair, the self-assessment can provide an opportunity to discuss problematic behavior and ways to modify it. The overall result, when this process is carried out with mutual respect, is a stronger board with members who have deeper awareness of their contributions, potential, and value to the whole organization.

USING PEER REVIEW

Some boards engage in peer evaluation as well as, or in place of, self-assessment. One organization incorporated peer review into a comprehensive evaluation regimen that it adopted as part of its strategic planning process. Members completed questionnaires on peer performance, which the governance committee analyzed, summarized, and translated into a board action plan. The plan included strengths to utilize more effectively, education to address gaps in board member effectiveness, and targeted recruiting to supply missing expertise.

The committee chair shared peer feedback with each member, and together they developed individual action plans for the coming year. Board members reported that the thorough process gave them a better understanding of their roles and the roles of other board members, as well as a greater appreciation for the value of their contributions.

When education and board member assessment do not resolve the issues with a problematic board member, the board can decide to simply rely on term limits, which provide a relatively painless way to rotate ineffective, inactive, or troublesome members off the board. If the board believes the member must leave before the term ends, however, the board chair may have to carry out board policies related to sanctioning or removing a board member.

Asking an ineffective or difficult board member to step down is never easy. This role falls to the board chair, not the chief executive; if the chair is the member in question, the task falls to the chair of the governance committee. It is wise to solicit the advice of legal counsel to guide all actions and ask a third party (preferably another board member) to be present when asking the problematic member to step down.

While these situations are difficult, action is always preferable to inaction. In this case, the organization's mission and future effectiveness are more important than fear of hurting the feelings of individual board members.

TURNOVER AS REVITALIZATION

No matter how good any board member is, the organization will need to replace that person at an appropriate time and in an appropriate way. Among the highest honors for any outstanding board member should be the opportunity to retire while leaving a legacy as someone who truly helped the organization.

Effective boards reframe turnover as revitalization. They

- tap veterans in myriad ways — for example, as mentors, coaches, orienters, members of task forces, and spirit builders on campaign teams

- intentionally focus time and attention on building relationships among current and former board members to promote an attitude of sharing what you know and what you learned

- deliberately introduce promising prospects to committees, task forces, study groups, and special projects, recognizing that doing so converts turnover into continuity

Chairs and chief executives of performing boards translate turnover of the board chair into opportunity through succession planning (see Chapter 3). Beyond insisting upon a succession plan as an operational practice, they manage the risk of re-forming as a group every time a new board is sworn in. Many organizations, for example, identify potential chairs early and prepare them for their role by providing various leadership opportunities.

A variation on succession planning translates turnover of officers and committee chairs into opportunities as well. A high-performing board frequently invites its members to express interest in leadership positions and state their preference for committee and task force assignments. It does not assume that the chair or chief executive knows every member's qualifications. Also, a high-performing board treats assessing the effectiveness of groups and individuals as opportunities to spot and develop assets. Committee chairs are prospectors intent upon finding their replacements with enough time to groom them. These boards realize that a nonprofit board represents a wealth of human resources from which to draw.

Flourishing nonprofit organizations have boards committed to directing not only the course of their organizations but also the dynamics of their own group. They resist losing momentum when terms of members and officers end. Instead, they deliberately attend to their own dynamics by taking ownership of their operations and their culture.

? QUESTIONS THE BOARD SHOULD ASK

1. Does the size of our board provide different perspectives for discussions and analysis while enabling all members to actively engage in our work?

2. Does the governance committee, in collaboration with the board chair and the chief executive, evaluate its own needs and priorities to determine the qualifications for prospective board members?

3. Is the governance committee active throughout the year, assessing strengths and weaknesses and identifying and recruiting the best possible prospects for election?

4. What criteria does the governance committee use to rigorously evaluate board members who are eligible for re-election? What evidence do we have that such criteria have been applied?

5. Do we have policies and procedures that ensure adequate turnover and renewal on the board?

6. Do we continually assess the effectiveness of board orientation and continuing education and make revisions?

7. How does our board gauge the potential contributions of its members and tap them for the greatest benefit to the organization?

8. How does our board address its own development?

CHAPTER 3

BOARD LEADERSHIP

Effective organizations recognize that good governance begins with people who can do the most to fulfill the organization's mission and ensure that a strategic approach is taken to develop the board's future leaders. They implement a transparent and participatory process that assesses future organizational needs as well as the competencies and interests of current board members.

Ideally, the board chair takes the lead on sustaining the interests, engagement, and abilities of board members, with the assistance of the chief executive. The governance committee, which is charged with maximizing the board's effectiveness, assists them both.

In high-performing organizations, the interdependent team of board chair and chief executive develops a close working partnership based on the three pillars of effective board leadership:

- a shared understanding of the organization's mission and vision, communicated to the board and staff, so that all have a common sense of where the organization is going and why

- a clear sense of roles and responsibilities that distinguish governance from management, so that board members do not carry out administrative functions that properly belong to the staff, and staff members do not adopt and implement major organizational policies without input and agreement from the board

- a relationship of trust and transparency that allows challenges to be addressed openly and managed constructively

The common element supporting these three pillars is ongoing communication between the board chair and the chief executive.

Constructive partnerships rely upon formal communication —
in the form of regularly scheduled meetings (when the chair and
the chief executive live in proximity to one another) or phone
calls (when they do not) — and informal communication — in
the form of e-mail messages and phone calls that alert the other
to news, ideas, concerns, and suggestions. Regular and
reciprocal communication, formal and informal, between chair
and chief executive improve the chances that issues will be
anticipated and miscommunication will be detected and
deflected early.

Frequent communication allows the board chair and the chief
executive to address and eliminate any confusion or friction
with regard to gray areas of organizational leadership. They
clarify roles and responsibilities by using written job
descriptions (see Appendix I), by establishing mutual
expectations and definitions around the traditional management–
governance distinctions, and by identifying tasks that benefit
from shared responsibility. The organization's goals guide their
discussion of these matters.

LIVING THE MISSION

"The board chair and chief executive — as the leadership team
— are the foremost stewards of the mission," writes Keith Timko
in "Living Your Mission: What's Behind the 17 Words?" (*Board
Member®*, August/September 2005). He continues, "The most
successful leadership teams find organizational approaches that
continually revisit and reaffirm the mission of the organization.
They find ways of inspiring passion for the mission,
communicating the organization's core purpose, and measuring
performance relative to the mission. In short, they find a way to
live their mission and to make it part of their organizational
DNA."

ROLES AND RESPONSIBILITIES OF THE CHAIR AND THE CHIEF EXECUTIVE

The board chair's responsibilities divide into two distinct yet
inseparable areas: board process and board tasks. Board process

applies to building a strong team, and board tasks refer to the board team's plan of work.

In close collaboration with the chief executive and the governance committee, the chair fosters team building by continuously educating board members, spotting leadership promise among them, and nurturing that promise by providing leadership opportunities and personal mentoring. The chair ensures that the work of the board is aligned with the strategic plan and addressed appropriately in partnership with the staff.

The chief executive's responsibilities are not so easily categorized, influenced as they are by what Robert Herman and Richard Heimovics label "strange loops and tangled hierarchies." Writing in *Executive Leadership in Nonprofit Organizations: New Starts for Shaping Board-Staff Dynamics* (Jossey-Bass, 1991), Herman and Heimovics include the changing skills and personalities of the board chair and board members among those loops and hierarchies. Whatever the variations, however, the chief executive's core responsibility is to lead the staff and manage the organization, along with

- monitoring the quality and effectiveness of the organization and individual programs

- developing future board and staff leadership

- engaging in financial stewardship of the organization, within parameters established by the board

- building external relations and advocacy

- supporting the board

While each board chair–chief executive relationship will produce a unique variation, the following table summarizes the general responsibilities of the two positions. For each key function, the board chair and the chief executive support one another in maintaining focus on the mission and ensuring that the organization operates in alignment with its values.

FUNCTION	BOARD CHAIR
POLICY AND PLANNING	Facilitates boards involvement in approving guiding principles, policies, and mission
BUDGET AND FINANCES	Guides board in approving and overseeing budget; oversees outside audits; ensures that the board holds ultimate responsibility for integrity of organization's finances
BOARD MEETINGS	Leads and facilitates board meetings
COMMITTEE WORK	Structures overall committee system; is ad hoc member of all committees
BOARD DEVELOPMENT	Leads development of a strong board; sets goals and expectations for the board; cultivates leadership in individual board members; makes board development a priority
BOARD RECRUITMENT AND ORIENTATION	Works with governance committee to identify and recruit new board members
BOARD ASSESSMENT	Ensures regular opportunities for board self-assessment; oversees comprehensive board assessment every two to three years
STAFF OVERSIGHT, COMPENSATION, EVALUATION	Oversees hiring, compensation, and evaluation of chief executive; ensures chief executive succession plan exists
FUNDRAISING AND DEVELOPMENT	Solicits contributions from board members and ensures all board members do their share
PUBLIC RELATIONS AND COMMUNICATIONS	Promotes the work of the organization and encourages board members to do so; speaks for the board when controversy or crisis arises

CHIEF EXECUTIVE	SHARED
Carries out mission; implements strategic plan; provides administrative support for board policymaking	Create policies and guidelines; develop mission and vision statements; outline organizational values.
Proposes budget to board; manages programs according to board-adopted financial policies and budget guidelines	N/A
Ensures that board members have meeting materials and needed information; attends meetings, except specific executive sessions	Develop meeting agenda.
Sits in on appropriate committee meetings; ensures that committee members have staff support and needed materials/information	Review committee system and individual committees to ensure alignment with mission and strategic goals
Shares appropriate information to keep board informed and educated	Keep all board members engaged in the work of the organization
Assists in identifying and cultivating new board members; works with governance committee to structure board orientation	Identify skills, expertise, and attributes needed for the board
Assists in development of board assessment process	Assess results and consider improvements in collaboration with governance committee
Oversees and evaluates all staff; sets staff salaries within budget constraints	N/A
Coordinates overall fundraising effort; ensures staff support for fundraising	Solicit contributions from outside donors; set the case for — and the amount of — a capital campaign based on determined strategic objectives
Official spokesperson for the organization; coordinates public relations and communications	With board and staff, develop message that conveys the organization's mission effectively and can be used consistently by board and staff

CHARACTERISTICS OF EFFECTIVE LEADERS

Healthy organizations are led by strong boards and a strong staff. Clear job descriptions help define the boundaries between the various positions. In addition to knowing what to do, the leaders must possess specific characteristics that enable them to effectively fulfill the position's requirements. The following attributes facilitate the chairs and chief executives in assuming their respective duties.

Effective board chairs

- accept the appointment only if they have the commitment, capacity, and time to do what the position demands

- are fair and objective and leave personal preferences outside of the boardroom

- walk the talk by following the same guidelines to which they expect other board members to adhere

- know how to facilitate a productive meeting; they manage to involve all participants in deliberation, fairly address controversial issues, and succeed in building consensus

- commit to work with the chief executive without micromanagement

- know the organization; they have an in-depth understanding of the organization's past and present, as well as its desired future

- seek ongoing opportunities to further develop their own skills

- maintain the integrity of the board process determined by the board and resolve conflicts among board members

Strong chief executives

- are secure enough to build and maintain a good working relationship with the board chair by willingly sharing good and bad news

- are flexible enough to accommodate different styles of leadership as board chairs change

- have the capacity to work effectively with the entire board by paying attention to the needs of individual board members

- dare to take initiative without constant reinforcement from the board

- know how to plan a good board meeting by sharing their personal daily perspectives while understanding the board's more detached view of the organization and its needs

- are effective communicators who know what is appropriate to share with the board and the staff

- are good friend-raisers and fundraisers for the organization because of their charisma and networking skills

Together, the board chair and the chief executive provide the vision, guidance, and hard work needed to keep the organization moving forward in achievement of its mission. Through constant communication and steady collaboration, they model a powerful working relationship for board members and staff, setting a tone that enables the organization to focus on serving and making a real difference in the community.

TIP

Formally evaluate board member performance before assigning leadership positions. Officer and committee chair positions should not be rewards for being a nice person but rather should be encouragement and recognition for demonstrated leadership.

DEVELOPMENT OF NEW LEADERSHIP

The chair, the chief executive, and the governance committee purposefully groom future leadership through a transparent and participatory process that includes

- seeking leadership qualities in board prospects

- providing mentors for new board members

- assigning board members to specific committees and task forces

- providing opportunities for training and self-assessment

Cultivating strong one-on-one relationships with each board member enables the board chair to assign committee chairmanships to appropriate members and to nurture their leadership skills. By matching the most capable board members with significant committee positions, the board chair, along with the chief executive and the rest of the board, can gain a better appreciation of those members' performance and commitment to the work of the organization. At the same time, the appointed board members start acquiring the knowledge and skills that will make them strong board leaders in the future.

A board without experienced leadership is often a group without direction. Every board needs to plan for officer succession: how to identify leadership qualities, elect the best candidates for the positions, train the officers for their roles, and ensure timely rotation.

An officer is a board member with extra duties. Most state laws require certain officers within each board. These roles are defined in the bylaws. The following positions are common in nonprofit boards, although they are not necessarily the most appropriate ones for every organization.

- **Board chair.** As the chief volunteer officer and role model for the board, this person has the most demanding task. The chair's primary responsibility is to develop the board as a cohesive and effective team.

- **Vice-chair.** This position fills in when the chair is not able to carry out the duties.

- **Chair-elect.** Essentially the chair-in-waiting, this position provides for automatic succession when the chair's term ends.

- **Treasurer.** This officer keeps the board up-to-date on the organization's finances.

- **Secretary.** The tasks of this position — to keep the minutes and the board records — are more and more often filled by a staff person rather than a board member. Some boards combine the positions of secretary and treasurer, specifying in their bylaws that one person is responsible for the respective duties.

Serving as an officer is an added responsibility but also provides an opportunity for a board member to show special commitment and improve personal leadership skills.

By matching the most capable board members with significant committee positions early on, the board and chief executive assess potential even as future leaders acquire the knowledge and skills for the future. Simultaneously, rising leaders get a taste of the demands and rewards of leadership, which helps them determine their continuing interest and capacity for future roles.

No matter how good board members are as leaders, they eventually need to be replaced at an appropriate time and in an appropriate way. Among the highest honors for any outstanding board member should be the opportunity to retire and be replaced by another equally qualified or even more remarkable member. The governance committee, the board chair, the chief executive, and board members should all have succession planning on their minds, to ensure that the right people are leading the organization at the right moment.

BOARD CHAIR SUCCESSION PLANNING

Through intentional leadership development, both the chair and the chief executive are ready — one to cede and the other to partner — when another member assumes the chair position. A nonprofit organization's bylaws guide the transfer of leadership by specifying officer term limits, and the board chair succession plan builds on that time frame. By the time the board chair has completed the first half of the term, steps should be underway to identify potential candidates as the next chair. Having a specific term limit for a board chair ensures that the board doesn't become too comfortable with one person's leadership.

Some boards create a chair-elect position, while others precede board chairmanship with chairmanship of the finance committee, development committee, or the annual campaign effort. Both approaches provide the prospective chair with valuable on-the-job training, increase familiarity with key people and salient facts about the organization, and contribute to building the relationship with the chief executive.

If, for some reason, no prospective board chair is in line, the board chair and chief executive should help the governance committee identify a successor. Working together, they can ensure that the unprepared successor receives substantial orientation, training, and mentoring.

CHIEF EXECUTIVE SUCCESSION PLANNING

The board and the chief executive also need to plan for a transition in the executive suite. No one stays in a job forever, so the board and chief executive should have a plan in place for filling the vacancy created by the chief executive's eventual departure. In fact, according to BoardSource's *Nonprofit Governance Index 2007*, 49 percent of the chief executives who responded anticipate leaving their positions within the next five years. That same survey, however, found that only 30 percent of their board members are expecting the chief executive's departure.

Although the list of board responsibilities includes selecting, supporting, and evaluating the chief executive, board members often interpret that as being applicable only after the current chief executive has announced plans to leave. Nonprofit parking lots are replete with stories of boards frantically reacting to the chief executive's resignation notice with avowals of support and promises of a long-overdue performance evaluation. Even boards with complete files of performance reviews and merit increases for their chief executives seem reluctant to prepare for this eventuality.

In fact, succession planning begins when the new chief executive arrives. Developing a systematic process and incorporating it into the board's chart of work creates an environment for a chief executive to succeed from the first day on the job to the last. By starting early and purposefully planning a process for replacing the chief executive, the incumbent chief executive, board chair, and board members can create the conditions for a smooth executive transition without feeling threatened or pressured.

Reviewing the process periodically — perhaps as part of the chief executive's annual evaluation — and revising it to meet changing circumstances not only keeps it current but also readies board members psychologically for a transition.

QUESTIONS THE BOARD SHOULD ASK

1. Do we fully understand the differences between board roles and responsibilities and staff roles and responsibilities?

2. How do the board chair and chief executive stay abreast of developments and challenges and convey that information to the board?

3. How do we encourage board members to recognize the opportunities — and be considered — for leadership positions? What criteria do we use to evaluate the appropriateness of members to positions?

4. If our chief executive resigned tomorrow, would we be prepared to implement a succession plan?

5. What succession plan do we currently have in place for the board chair?

CHAPTER 4

COMMITTEE STRUCTURE

Effective organizations keep their board meetings focused on strategy and course corrections. Much of the roll-up-your-sleeves work gets accomplished at the committee or task force level.

Many nonprofit organizations that used to favor large boards with multiple standing committees, plus an executive committee with substantial responsibility, have moved to a more streamlined structure of smaller boards with fewer standing committees supplemented by task forces to address specific issues or concerns. This move provides a more flexible board structure: The board can promptly respond to changing circumstances and match task forces to the goals and objectives set out in the organization's strategic plan.

PITFALL

If you downsize your board without an equivalent restructuring of committees and a revision of member expectations, fatigue or burnout is sure to occur. A reduced board membership cannot support or serve on the same number of committees as its larger precursor.

COMMITTEES AND TASK FORCES

Each organization's board establishes the structure of committees and task forces that will best help it carry out its work and achieve its goals. That structure depends on both the size and capabilities of the organization's staff and the directions and priorities set by the organization's strategic plan.

Committees. Generally part of the overall board structure, a committee is commissioned with a specific charge and may be stipulated in the bylaws. Standing committees are permanent; they deal with matters that involve a continuous flow of work, such as financial oversight or board development. Committee members are appointed for designated terms.

Nonprofit boards are moving away from maintaining structures that mirror staff duties. For example, if an organization has a marketing staff, a board marketing committee may not be necessary. If the board includes marketing experts, marketing staff can certainly ask for advice, but the main marketing effort should be a staff responsibility. If, however, the organization has a small (or no) marketing staff because of its own size, the board chair may choose to appoint a task force to develop and carry out a marketing strategy for a designated period of time.

Another alternative would be to form an organizational committee composed of staff, external volunteers with specialized skills, and board members to guide marketing efforts. This team could develop a marketing plan and assign tasks to its members according to capability and capacity, while remaining fully cognizant that the committee was supporting operations and not addressing governance issues.

Task Forces. A task force is established to accomplish a specific objective, such as reviewing bylaws or planning a retreat, and then dissolves once it has completed its task.

The board chair appoints task forces as needed to address time-limited tasks with narrowly defined objectives. In particular, task forces are ideal for dealing with controversial or highly charged issues, such as changing fee structures for the organization's services or streamlining board structures. They also work well for naturally short-lived projects, such as strategic planning, executive searches, and board retreats.

Relying upon small groups to accomplish strategic priorities not only gets work done efficiently and effectively but also engages board members and invests them in the work of the board. In an article for the *Harvard Business Review,* Barbara Taylor, Richard Chait, and Thomas Holland note that these "'tissue paper' task forces (use and discard) drive the board toward real-time results, multiply leadership opportunities, and prevent longtime members from dominating standing committees."

BOARD AND ORGANIZATIONAL COMMITTEES

Board committees report to the board and help carry out its mandate to oversee the organization, ensure its financial security, and plan for its future. Board committees generally do not include staff members (except, in some cases, the chief executive), though they are often supported by staff.

Organizational committees report to staff members and help with operational issues, such as organizing special events to raise funds or planning new benefits for the membership. Organizational committees consist of both staff and board members and may also include outside experts. Board members serving on organizational committees serve as advisors to the staff and may also assist staff members with their work.

The board chair and the chief executive ensure that every board committee and task force has a clear statement of its overall purpose. Committees should set annual objectives for themselves in consultation with the board chair and the chief executive, as well as develop meeting schedules that relate to the timing of their regular responsibilities. Task forces should develop timelines and action plans for achieving their designated tasks. Written descriptions of objectives, roles, responsibilities, and authority help members of committees and task forces focus their attention properly and conduct their affairs appropriately.

The board chair is often responsible for appointing committee chairs, but some boards also include the full board in this decision. Identifying committee members can fall to the board chair, chief executive, committee chair, or other board members. A joint effort by the leadership that invites signs of interest from all board members but handpicks members of committees and task forces is one option — although somewhat time-consuming because it yields a variety of prospects for each work group. This approach also generates a sense of ownership of the group's work and commitment to its success.

The membership of a committee or task force may include non-board members as expert advisors, as well as "board members in training" who provide fresh perspectives. Members of committees and task forces are bound by the same ethical and moral standards as full-fledged board members, even if they do not have the authority to make organizational decisions.

TIP

When choosing committee members, don't focus only on apparent expertise or professional affiliation, such as appointing a CPA to the finance committee or a business owner to the strategic planning task force. Sometimes, bringing together different types of individuals (engineers and artists, for example, or businesspeople and homemakers), forms creative tension and may bring up questions that otherwise would remain unasked.

ESSENTIAL STANDING COMMITTEES

Many boards regard several board committees as essential, in particular those focusing on the board's own development and the organization's financial and ethical integrity. According to BoardSource's *Nonprofit Governance Index 2007,* the most common standing committees are governance, finance, and executive.

GOVERNANCE COMMITTEE

The governance committee serves as the board's mechanism for looking after itself. It addresses board composition, the roles and responsibilities of board members, board member knowledge, board leadership, and board effectiveness. Its charge is to find accomplished, enthusiastic people with the assets needed by the board; to teach these high performers what it means to be on the organization's board and continually engage them in its work; to evaluate the work of the board and each member's contribution, watching for leadership potential; and to make sure that the board is living up to its potential. To fulfill this charge, the committee

- identifies skills and areas of expertise needed by the board, based on the organization's mission and strategic plan

- actively seeks out, cultivates, and recruits board prospects, encouraging all board members to contribute ideas, connections, and time to this effort

- recommends individuals for election to the board or prepares a slate of candidates, as mandated by organization type and bylaws

- provides orientation and mentoring for new board members

- works with the board chair and the chief executive to promote ongoing learning and growth of all board members, keep board members engaged by involving them in work that matches their skills and interests, and actively encourage development of leadership potential

- assesses board member participation, commitment, and contribution to governance duties and considers suitability for re-election

- spearheads the board's self-assessment every few years

- evaluates and recommends necessary changes to the board structure, processes, and guiding documents (bylaws, policies)

- assesses its own performance

The future of the board and the future of the organization depend on the quality and skills of the people who serve on and lead the board. If the governance committee nominates, elects, and trains the right people, the organization is more likely to thrive. On the other hand, people who are not a good fit with the organization's mission or have inappropriate motivations for serving can significantly dilute the board's value and effectiveness.

The governance committee is more active and dynamic than its traditional precursor, the nominating committee. Rather than focusing on nominations for annual elections, the governance committee works year-round to guarantee that the board takes responsibility for its own development, learning, and behavior; sets and enforces its own expectations; and allots time, attention, and resources to understanding its stewardship role. These hefty demands require an astute chair leading a committee with a variety of expertise and connections, capable of maintaining confidences, and prepared to evaluate peers objectively.

FINANCE AND AUDIT COMMITTEES

The finance committee enables the board to carry out its fiduciary responsibility by overseeing the fiscal health of the organization. Boards need to observe due diligence and appropriate processes in regard to investment strategies, vendor contracts, contributions from major donors, and all organizational purchases and expenses.

Because these financial concepts may not be intuitive for the majority of board members, nonprofit organizations depend upon finance committees to

- understand issues of financial integrity and solvency and explain them to the board

- work with staff to develop proposed budgets for consideration and adoption by the full board

- monitor income and expenses against the annual budget

- work with staff to provide up-to-date financial statements to the board

- ensure that financial practices follow state and federal laws

- recognize signs of financial trouble and act on them appropriately

- work with staff to establish internal controls and procedures that protect the organization

- advise the board on the feasibility of proposed activities and strategies, given the organization's fiscal status

- ensure that the IRS Form 990 (or 990-EZ or 990-PF) is completed and signed by the chief executive or chief financial officer and reviewed by the board before filing

In the past, nonprofit organizations often relied upon the finance committee to also serve as the audit committee. The passage of the Sarbanes-Oxley Act has led many nonprofits to recognize the value of a separate audit committee that can be more objective than the finance committee, which is involved in the organization's accounting, might be. The complexity of financial transactions in many major organizations also makes it necessary to delegate the monitoring of various aspects of the organization's finances to separate groups that possess the needed expertise.

The audit committee identifies the type of audit needed and determines the frequency with which audits should be conducted. It recommends audit firms to the board and provides guidance on how often to rotate the firm. The committee should also ensure that the full board has an opportunity to meet privately with the auditor at the end of the audit process.

Particularly in organizations with permanent endowments or sizable investments in general, it may make sense to form a separate investment committee. This committee would not become involved in the actual portfolio management but would draft the overall investment policies and choose and monitor the performance of an outside investment manager.

EXECUTIVE COMMITTEE

The executive committee is a small group that has authority to act on behalf of the full board between meetings or in an urgent situation. Usually the executive committee includes the board chair and other board officers. Committee chairs may also sit on the executive committee, and the chief executive serves as an ex officio member. If the executive committee is allowed to act on behalf of the board, its membership, functions, and authority level must be specifically stated in the organization's bylaws.

Not all nonprofit organizations need an executive committee. Small boards and the boards of start-up organizations rarely do, for instance, because all board members can be convened relatively easily and need to be involved in decision making. For large and/or geographically dispersed boards, the existence of an executive committee whose membership can be convened quickly and make decisions efficiently may prove critical in emergency situations. However, the full board — not the executive committee alone — should always make significant decisions such as amending the bylaws, electing or removing board members, hiring or firing the chief executive, and approving the budget.

An executive committee has two inherent dangers:

- Because a smaller group is more efficient, the board may be inclined to delegate responsibilities to the executive committee that are properly handled by the full board.

- When a select group handles many of the major deliberations and decisions, other board members may begin to feel underutilized, unwanted, or disenfranchised.

Recognizing these dangers, some nonprofit organizations have amended their bylaws to eliminate the executive committee as a standing committee of the board. Others have refined the executive committee's role so that it carries out specific functions, such as the performance review of the chief executive, that are best handled by a small, knowledgeable group that can act efficiently and maintain confidentiality.

Still others have redefined the executive committee's role significantly. One board, for example, recast its executive committee as a strategic think tank for the board itself, not to make decisions in the board's place. Comprised of committee vice-chairs, this redefined executive committee models a think tank practice for all other committees to emulate.

ADVISORY COUNCILS AND EMERITUS POSITIONS

Many boards enlarge their organization's reach by including advisory councils: groups of people who agree to either provide expertise or technical assistance when needed or simply participate in volunteer activities, such as fundraising, to help the board function more effectively. Such councils do not necessarily meet on their own, but members may be available individually and in small groups for consultation.

When a board incorporates such ancillary groups, it can avoid confusion by labeling them "councils" instead of "boards." The term "board" implies decision-making authority and ultimate accountability. But these groups normally serve an advisory rather than a governing function.

The advisory councilor role can serve as a stepping stone to board membership — a good way for potential members to get to know the organization and for the board to see if those advisors might be a good fit for board service. Advisory councils can also engage prominent community leaders who might not be willing to devote the time and attention required of governing board members.

More commonly, boards form advisory groups so board members can continue their affiliation with the organization after their terms have concluded. Emeritus positions also provide an opportunity to honor long-serving board members whose terms have expired but who remain vital to the future of the organization. One organization, for instance, appoints one of its emeritus members to serve as the board's historian.

Emeritus members may receive the mailings sent to regular board members and occasional invitations to meetings. Many of them serve actively as full members of committees. They do not, however, have a vote in regular meetings of the governing board.

TIP

Guard against having too many non-board members around the table at each board meeting because this hampers effective discussions — especially those related to charting new directions.

It may be wise to limit a person's emeritus tenure and the number of people serving in this capacity. While it's important to encourage new people and ideas on a board, those needs must be balanced with the preservation of organizational memory. Using former board members as advisors or committee members may be a more practical way to benefit from their expertise than inviting them to regularly participate in board meetings.

EVALUATING AND RESTRUCTURING COMMITTEES AND TASK FORCES

Many nonprofit boards regularly evaluate and revise the structure of their committees and task forces. Doing so helps to ensure that committees do not outlive their reasons for coming into existence, have tasks assigned to them that are not really their responsibility, or begin pursuing initiatives and carrying out activities that the board has not considered and approved. It also encourages the board to connect the organization's strategic plan with action by defining the roles and timelines of committees and task forces in relation to plan accomplishment.

Some boards adopt a zero-based committee structure to keep their committees purposeful, efficient, and relevant. With a zero-based structure, the board starts from zero — with no committees or task forces in place — every year (or every other year). After identifying its needs and strategic priorities for the year, the board sets up the structure of committees and task forces that will best respond to those priorities.

This approach may sound drastic, but it helps combat stagnation and the force of habit. Some boards have adopted a hybrid system in which they maintain a few standing committees over time and use the zero-based approach for all other committees. This allows them to combine needed continuity with opportunities for revitalization.

QUESTIONS THE BOARD SHOULD ASK

1. Do all committees, task forces, or groups charged with activities on behalf of the board have current, written, and approved descriptions and charts of work?

2. What standing committees might we eliminate in favor of assigning their functions to task forces?

3. Is the audit function sufficiently independent to ensure objectivity?

4. What elements of our strategic plan align with our structures (committees, task forces, etc.)? Is this the most efficient and effective organizational approach for meeting our plan's specifics?

5. Has our system for recruiting and developing board members yielded the quality, mix, and dynamism demanded by the environment in which our organization operates? Do we need to refine our processes?

CHAPTER 5

BOARD MEETINGS

Why do boards underperform in meetings? The two most common reasons, identified by Richard Chait, Thomas Holland, and Barbara Taylor in their research on nonprofit boards, are "no red meat on the table" and "no light at the end of the tunnel." In other words, board members feel unproductive when they have no significant issues or decisions to address and when they believe their contributions don't make a difference to the organization.

The faster pace of society and the presence of younger and more assertive board members have pushed boards to streamline their structures and operations, including meetings. Busy executives and energetic young professionals want to get in, get the job done, and move on. But board action happens only in board meetings — the "official venue" for decision making. As a result, each board needs to strike an appropriate balance that will ensure fast-paced, efficient meetings while maintaining the spirit of teamwork and collegiality among board members. The collegial spirit can disappear when meetings become too structured, but valuable board members may leave if they feel their time is not used productively.

Achieving the all-important balance requires careful organization and preparation for board meetings. The most effective boards plan their meetings to focus on the important matters of governance while preserving the sense of community and mission that brings the organization together. Operating efficiently should allow more time, not less, for personal interaction among board members to build mutual understanding and respect. Dealing with issues that allow board members to use their skills and expertise makes board meetings more informative and interesting, thus providing a bigger incentive to attend and participate in them.

SMALL STEPS, BIG RESULTS

Attention to simple details — such as congenial seating arrangements, incorporating icebreakers to learn more about members, and group work to design solutions — can reap remarkable returns. For example, the board of the Lake Champlain Committee, a two-state environmental advocacy organization, literally gives members different perspectives by rotating meetings between New York and Vermont.

PLANNING THE MEETING

Successful board meetings begin with an annual plan that establishes the year's meeting schedule so that all members know in advance when and where meetings will take place and what they will cover. Some organizations set their meetings as much as three years in advance, to give busy board members plenty of time to clear their calendars and avoid scheduling conflicts.

Setting up a yearly meeting calendar should include taking time to determine if a meeting requires the full board's presence or if other groups (task forces, committees) can handle the business. Some procedures and issues must be covered at specific times, and scheduling them on an annual calendar of meetings enables the board and staff to plan accordingly.

State laws usually require that a nonprofit board hold at least one meeting annually, but the boards of most organizations meet more frequently because one meeting per year hardly allows the board to pay proper attention to its fiduciary duties. The frequency of board meetings (monthly, bimonthly, quarterly) can depend on several factors, from geography and function to the board's life cycle and capacity to whether the organization is local, national, or international in scope. Some boards, for example, need enough time between their meetings to engage in committee or task force work and to review relevant reports related to upcoming board action items.

The amount of work to be accomplished in alignment with the organization's strategic plan will influence the frequency of meetings. When the organization has a very small staff and a "working board," or when the organization faces a crisis situation, meetings may need to take place monthly or on an as-needed basis. On the other hand, some boards may meet monthly even when such frequency is not necessary, either because committees and task forces do not function as they should or because the board has simply gotten in the habit of meeting every four weeks. These boards should have a serious discussion on the purpose of their meetings.

To determine how frequently the board needs to meet,

- develop an annual plan that assigns board tasks and functions to the time of year when they need to happen. For instance, the board will need to approve the budget before the organization's fiscal year begins and review the audit results several months after the fiscal year ends. This scheduling enables all board members to see what contributions they will need to make and when.

- assign routine functions that are not time sensitive — such as review of bylaws and policies or review of liability exposure and insurance coverage — to specific meetings as well, so that they are not all left until the last meeting of the year. Through this process, the board chair and chief executive may determine that some tasks can be handled by committees and task forces between meetings, reducing the need for the full board to meet.

MEETINGS WITH PURPOSE

One Midwestern board has found that committing three agendas a year to single topics increases participation and energy, paves the way for breakthrough ideas, and enables untapped leadership to surface. Generative questions, sent before the meeting, prepare members for these high-energy sessions, which are characterized by a healthy tension that facilitates collective and individual growth.

Another board commits a portion of every board meeting to an in-depth look at a particular topic; this provides useful knowledge for carrying out strategy.

An organization might, for example, devote one meeting per year to basic board operating functions, including election of new members and board officers and the review of program evaluations and financial reports from the previous year. This meeting might also include a review of and adjustments to committee and task force memberships, as well as a presentation by a motivational speaker or governance consultant.

In between face-to-face meetings, if the state laws allow it, some boards may meet via conference call to cut costs and address specific items of business. The basic meeting requirements do not change: It is necessary to establish a quorum, allow everyone to express opinions, keep track of the flow of the meeting and voting results, and produce accurate minutes. The facilitator's role in this type of meeting is more complicated, but as long as all members understand the guidelines, this format can be a convenient way to encourage participation when board members aren't in the same place.

MEETING VIA CONFERENCE CALL

Telephone conferences can be a cost-effective way to convene a meeting when board members are geographically dispersed or need to make a quick decision. Following these guidelines will ensure that all board members have equal opportunities to interact and contribute to the discussion.

- Prepare board members for the meeting. Communicate the meeting's purpose, and set a starting time that is convenient for all participants, taking different time zones into account. Make sure that everybody receives the necessary background information before the meeting.

- Ask all participants to call from a quiet location to minimize background noise.

- Begin the meeting with a roll call to ensure you have a quorum.

- Ask participants to identify themselves when speaking. This also facilitates accurate minute-taking.

- Create a participatory dynamic by calling on any members whose voices have not yet been heard during the meeting.

- As in all meetings, enforce the rule that only one person should speak at a time.

Very few states allow boards to meet via e-mail, which can raise issues about confidentiality. E-mail communication between meetings may facilitate sharing of documents or making announcements, but voting electronically on issues generally is not a good process for boards. Board members need to interact with each other directly. By observing and listening to one another's opinions, individual board members form their own positions on issues. Deliberation is an essential part of educated and wise decision making without compromising confidentiality or inviting board members to form opinions in a vacuum.

PREPARING FOR THE MEETING

Successful board meetings begin long before the board chair calls the meeting to order. The chief architects of the meetings, the board chair and the chief executive, should shape each meeting around the answers to two questions:

- What is the purpose of this meeting?

- How can we organize the meeting to fulfill that purpose?

Preparation includes establishing the time and place of the meeting, confirming it with board members, determining the issues to be covered, preparing and providing background information, and preparing and circulating draft proposals for action so board members have time to gather the information they need to determine their initial positions. Board members should receive these materials at least one week before the meeting takes place.

Agenda. The board chair and the chief executive work together to develop a meeting agenda that includes both the board chair's big picture view with a focus on governance and the chief executive's updates on the organization, industry trends, and community issues. To increase efficiency and ensure that they address important issues, many organizations have adopted a format that opens with a consent agenda, followed by substantive matters in order of importance.

A consent agenda groups together non-contested items that require board action but not discussion or debate — such as approval of meeting minutes, acceptance of reports from committees and the chief executive, and final approval of other items that the board has previously deliberated upon. Using a consent agenda reduces the amount of time a board must dedicate to handling routine matters, allowing it to meaningfully discuss initiatives that will shape organizational strategy and actions.

All board members should receive the written materials for the consent agenda before the meeting so they have time to review the items and be prepared to approve them as a group, without discussion. The consent agenda is the first item voted upon during the meeting. The chair should ask if any items in the package require discussion; if so, the chair withdraws those items from the consent agenda for later discussion. With all controversial items removed, the board can approve the package and then move on to the rest of the meeting agenda, which should contain two types of items:

- discussion items that share information or pose big-picture, what-if questions and ask for board members' input

- action items that convey information, knowledge, or data and require a board decision or vote. Examples include voting on the annual budget and setting strategic planning goals. Any printed material related to action items must be sent ahead to all board members so they can prepare accordingly.

Ideally, items should appear on the agenda in order of importance, not history, with top-priority items coming first. Most meetings have one or two items that require special attention, yet all too often these appear late on the agenda, when board members have started closing their notebooks to leave.

The estimated amount of time allotted for each item can also help guide the meeting's pace. Some organizations list the phone number of the board member responsible for an agenda item, so any member who needs more information after reading the meeting materials can call. This eliminates redundant questions during the meeting itself, enabling the board chair to keep everyone focused on the most important or complex issues.

Reports. All reports, including those submitted by committees, should be written and circulated in advance. This gives board members time to review the reports and formulate the questions they'd like to ask at the meeting. It does not give board members an excuse to ignore the information or provide the means for a small group to slip something past the full board.

Only reports that directly influence decisions on the agenda need to be presented orally at the meeting itself. Some reports might be updates — if, for example, the organization has a fundraising campaign underway or is engaged in negotiations to purchase or sell a property — while other reports would be included in the consent agenda and require no discussion. Only the action items call for oral transmission and deliberation.

Proposals for Board Action. Too often, proposals for major board action are conceived, constructed, articulated, and approved during board meetings. This process wastes valuable meeting time and usually produces inadequate policies that are expressed in poorly worded motions.

For a simple solution, have individuals, committees, or task forces prepare and distribute policy proposals in advance of board meetings using a standard template (see Appendix II). The discipline of writing the proposal forces the author to word the motion carefully — and helps avoid endless wordsmithing during the meeting.

Furthermore, this process enables the person who takes the minutes to record motions exactly as presented. This accuracy is essential because, regardless of what the board intended when passing a motion, the written record as printed in the minutes is the official motion. Motions must be written in a way that will have meaning for future boards as well as the current board.

ADVANCE PREPARATION OF AGENDA TOPICS

The Project Management Institute, a global professional membership association, requires completion of a template for all board agenda topics (see Appendix II). The template calls for a write-up of the motion or other outcome, context, impact on stakeholders, business analysis, communication plan, and any supporting information. The template becomes the record regardless of the action.

During the board meeting, board members discuss every agenda topic and, if a motion is included, take a straw poll. If the results indicate division, a small group takes the proposal, refines it, and brings it back for another straw poll, which can lead to a formal motion and a vote. The process, though lengthy, engages the whole board in thoughtful work, educates members, and builds buy-in to the final outcome.

Policy Compendium. Board members and staff rarely know the policy history of the organization, and sometimes they initiate new proposals that contradict or duplicate existing policies. To avoid this trap, the organization could create a compendium of all policies ever adopted by the board. The compendium should include an index to facilitate location of existing policies on any subject.

A task force, a volunteer, or an intern can undertake this process, ideally producing an electronic product that is searchable and easily updated. Once the compendium is complete, board members can research the history and current policies on any subject before presenting new policy proposals.

TIP

When a board has its own password-protected Web site, board members can easily access and review the organization's bylaws, most recent Form 990, most recent audit, calendar of upcoming meetings, minutes of previous meetings, committee and staff rosters, committee reports, the manual of board policies, and so forth.

Dashboards. Just as an automobile dashboard offers the driver a status report on key functions at a glance, a nonprofit dashboard provides a synopsis of the organization's "vital signs." In a graphic format, dashboards show nonprofit boards where the organization is thriving and where it is struggling at a given point in time.

A single page included in the board book distributed before each meeting helps board members arrive with an indication of areas that may require special attention. Indicators might include historic comparisons and relationships with budgets and plans. Financial indicators might show year-to-date donations compared with budget projections and receipts at the same time a year ago. Similarly, rates of participation or attendance for programs or services can be presented in an easily understood graphic format.

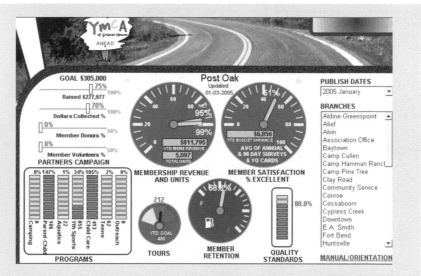

The Houston YMCA inserts its key indicators into a mock car dashboard and posts the privileged data on its Web site reserved for board members. Board members can see the big picture through the "dials," which indicate progress to date by dollars, donors, and volunteers in an annual fundraising campaign as well as membership by unit, dollars, satisfaction, and retention.

Productive meetings require careful preparation as well as skillful implementation. By relying on consent agendas to handle routine items with one vote and dashboards to focus on institutional performance, capacity, and condition, boards have more time for strategizing and learning conversations that expand board members' understanding, stimulate creative solutions, and build enthusiasm. Intentionally productive practices respect members' time and intelligence and allow them to devote precious meeting time to dynamic interaction.

TIPS FOR GOOD BOARD MEETINGS

- Develop an agenda that focuses the discussion on strategic topics.

- Start on time and end on time.

- Don't allow people to go off the subject.

- Create time for board learning.

- Encourage everyone to feel comfortable speaking up.

- Keep things moving. If something comes up that can't be resolved today, don't dwell on it. Say you'll put it on the agenda for the next meeting.

- Have a sense of humor!

CHAIRING THE MEETING

The role of facilitating the board meeting usually falls to the chair (or vice-chair, when necessary). The chair makes sure that the agenda fits the meeting and that the board members fulfill their roles and responsibilities to achieve the objectives set out on the agenda. The chair also sets the tone, the pace, and the process for board meetings. The goal is to ensure that members feel welcome, participate, and spend their time together productively by focusing on action and decision making.

To enable the board to make knowledgeable decisions, the board chair and chief executive can use provocative questions to prompt thoughtful discussion. They don't rush deliberation.

They also incorporate executive sessions with and without the presence of the chief executive — not to escape difficult dialogue but to encourage frank discussion of confidential issues.

The bylaws of most organizations indicate that meetings should follow *Robert's Rules of Order.* Few board members, however, have ever read these rules — and if they had, they probably would not have thought them appropriate for their boards. In fact, *Robert's Rules* were developed for a large parliamentary setting where representatives look out for the constituents who elected them and do whatever is necessary to gain acceptance of their opinions. In such a setting, careful attention to process is necessary to guard against tyranny of the loudest and endless arguments over procedure.

Every nonprofit board meeting needs a framework, defined processes, and order, and the use of basic parliamentary procedure can keep things moving forward. But a nonprofit board meeting should focus on discussion and deliberation rather than structuring every expression into a specific order. In other words, each board should adopt a system of rules that still allows for flexibility. The rules should free the board chair to guide deliberation in a manner that invites open discussion and creative solutions. The board chair determines when all opinions have been heard and the group is ready to vote, puts the motion back on the table, and records the results.

Unless its bylaws stipulate the use of *Robert's Rules of Order,* a board should determine what rules and procedures it intends to follow for meeting management. At a minimum, rules should include

- determining whether a quorum is present
- declaring when the meeting starts and adjourns
- making and seconding motions
- allowing the chair to facilitate discussion and make judgment calls when order is lost or unruly members dominate the floor
- reaching a general understanding of procedure when an impasse occurs

PITFALL

When a board insists upon strict adherence to parliamentary procedure, it risks becoming more involved and interested in the nitty-gritty details of making motions and amendments rather than in the substantive issues being discussed and decided. A board's system of rules should be flexible enough to allow for dialogue and idea generation.

ATTENDING THE MEETING

Board members must take meeting attendance seriously and make it a priority. They must attend board meetings to fulfill their duty of care — a legal obligation that defines the attention, thought, and consideration they must exercise in their role as guardians of the organization (see Chapter 2).

Additionally, board members who miss meetings can affect the board's ability to have a quorum. State law often defines a quorum as a majority of voting members; an organization's bylaws may set a higher standard. Without a quorum, the meeting is not official and the decisions made cannot be regarded as binding on the organization.

While this legal consideration is significant, many board members do not find it particularly compelling. Ultimately, board members convene because they have developed positive working relationships with one another and believe their participation is essential to maximizing the board's assets. Board members attend because the meetings matter to them and they feel they matter to the meetings.

In addition to board members, the chief executive naturally attends the entire meeting. The chief executive is usually, but not always, an ex officio member of the board, having a seat and a voice but no vote. The decision on whether or not to make the chief executive a voting member of the board is individual to each organization. According to BoardSource's *Nonprofit Governance Index 2007,* only 14 percent of the responding organizations include the chief executive as a voting member of the board.

IMPROVING MEETING ATTENDANCE AND ENJOYMENT

- Make attendance as effortless as possible by setting dates, sites, and expectations a year or two ahead.

- Send meeting materials in advance, in the print or electronic format that each board member prefers.

- Follow up meeting notices with personal phone calls from the chair that encourage attendance and provide specifics on what the chair feels the board member will be able to contribute. For example, "I'll be glad to have you there, Jane. Your expertise in commercial real estate will be invaluable as we discuss options for moving to a larger facility."

- Allow time for personal contact and informal socializing.

- Conduct quick evaluations after every meeting, perhaps via a brief Web-based survey, with the goal of making each meeting more productive and satisfying than the last.

- Remind board members why they joined the board by holding meetings in a program facility where they can see the organization in action.

As an example of the last strategy, a 100-year-old family service organization held a legacy event to honor a founder of its long-running camp. Board members attended alongside past and present members, volunteers, and staff. They also listened to tales of a school bus that had once transported children to camp and had been purchased with Green Stamps — bonus coupons awarded by various stores that could be redeemed for merchandise.

The legacy event achieved two results: It laid the groundwork for re-engaging former leadership in building an endowment, and it generated a greater sense of responsibility and heritage among current board members. As a result, the board's governance committee revisited its plan of work.

During the board meeting, the chief executive provides the insider perspective and information on the organization's activities and their outcomes, ongoing needs, and opportunities for growth or further outreach. This enhances the board's ability to deliberate and make informed decisions.

Other staff members usually don't attend the entire meeting, only those portions that relate to their areas of expertise or require the sharing of information relevant to specific agenda items. Although it can make chief executives and boards nervous, structured staff participation in board meetings enhances staff morale and helps build strong board–staff relationships. Having staff present also makes it possible to quickly answer board questions or verify details about finances, programs, and other issues for which the senior staff is responsible.

 TIP

Make sure staff members do not outnumber board members at meetings, and minimize staff time on the agenda to prevent influencing the amount, opportunity, and direction of discussion that rightfully belong to the board. Also establish a procedure for when staff should come and go during board meetings to minimize disruption.

The chair may invite other non-board members to attend, depending on their possible contributions to the meeting (speakers and subject matter experts, such as a lawyer or parliamentarian) or their interest in the organization (funders, facilitators, and constituents). Some boards openly encourage attendance by outsiders. If a board runs its meetings under sunshine laws — that is, the meetings must be open to the public — it should plan for outsiders' attendance.

MEETING MINUTES

Meeting minutes provide an official record of board actions. They report what was done; they do not serve as a verbatim transcript of the meeting. Once approved at a subsequent meeting, minutes become legal documents, and policies indicated in the minutes as approved become official policy.

Approved policies and adopted motions remain in effect until superseded or rescinded at a future board meeting. Board members, staff, or attorneys reading the minutes decades later should be able to discern the meaning from the minutes themselves, not from the vague recollections of people who may have attended the meeting. Using templates for action items simplifies the wording of motions and insertion into minutes in clear unambiguous language that will continue to have meaning long after the chair has adjourned the meeting.

Minutes should be written carefully, accurately, and concisely. Depending on the organization's culture, the board may choose the minutes of its meetings to reflect the following:

- a brief synopsis of the reports presented

- any proposals or motions for board approval

- the names of the board members making and seconding the motions

- a brief summary of the discussion leading to a vote on a motion (if it adds to the understanding of the motion and the context within which it was approved or rejected)

- the names and votes of those voting for, against, and abstaining, particularly if a roll call vote is requested

- the convening and purpose (but not the actual content) of an executive session

EXECUTIVE SESSIONS

When the board needs to discuss confidential or sensitive issues, the board chair should call for an executive session. Additionally, the board chair should clarify if other board members can request an executive session — and how to do so.

The issue being discussed will determine who participates in an executive session. Normally, all board members are present. The chief executive is present if the issue does not relate to the chief executive; others who have relevant information to contribute may participate at the invitation of the chair. Only board members would participate in an executive session devoted to discussing the chief executive's performance review and compensation. Similarly, an executive session with the auditor does not include any staff.

Some boards have an executive session without the chief executive at every meeting to establish the habit and procedure. Establishing this pattern can help avoid a crisis of trust if a problem does arise — no one feels uncomfortable, startled, or surprised by the board meeting in an executive session. In addition, these sessions give board members uninterrupted time to talk to one another.

Another type of executive session focuses on what Keeps the President Awake at Night (KPAWN). It devotes perhaps 15 minutes to the issues of greatest concern to the chief executive. This not only enables the chief executive to release pressure without judgment but also gives the board a better understanding of and appreciation for the chief executive's responsibilities.

Usually, in an executive session, the conversation remains confidential and is not recorded in the minutes. The purpose of the session must be established ahead of time; the minutes of the board meeting should indicate the time when the board met in executive session, the purpose of the session, who was present, and a list of any actions taken or decisions made.

Because nonvoting participants in a board meeting will be asked to leave when an executive session begins, it is best to schedule the executive session just before a break or at the end of a board meeting. An organization's bylaws or board policies should spell out the procedures, which also warrant review during board member orientation.

TIP

If board members often have questions about the information they receive from the chief executive — whether during or in between meetings — add a meeting discussion topic on what board members actually want and what format they prefer. Having consensus on this issue also helps the chief executive fine-tune the report's function and eliminate or expand some aspects of it.

EVALUATING THE MEETING

To be productive, board meetings need to matter. As the agent for board effectiveness, the governance committee assumes responsibility for evaluating meetings and, in discussion with the board chair, recommending improvements. Investing a few minutes at the end of each meeting to ask board members what went well (and what didn't) can reap a substantial return. (See Appendix IV for a sample evaluation form, which can easily be adapted to a Web-based survey and e-mailed to board members a few days after a meeting.)

The evaluations need not be personal or critical. They can gather valuable feedback for the next meeting by asking such questions as

- Did this meeting deal with substantive issues of strategic import to our board?

- Did the advance materials and reports provide the information you needed to make informed decisions?

- Did the chair keep the meeting on time and focused on the written agenda?

- Was ample time allowed for discussion and deliberation of each agenda item?

- Did this meeting use your time and talents wisely?

RETREATS

A board's calendar of meetings should include an annual retreat, which gives the board an opportunity to gather away from the usual meeting place. A change in location encourages board members to step away from ingrained patterns of thinking and open themselves to new ideas and different perspectives. And, in addition to the change of space, a retreat offers a change of pace; it gives the board time to reflect and exchange ideas on one major topic without the demands and distractions of a regular meeting.

The board chair should participate in planning the retreat, which a special task force or committee (generally the governance committee) may spearhead. Board members should arrive at the retreat thoroughly informed of its purpose and objectives and prepared to contribute to a successful outcome.

Retreats have many uses. For example, a retreat may focus on

- the board's role in the organization
- board self-assessment
- reflection on mission and vision
- a specific challenge (recruitment, fundraising)
- strategic issues and goals
- scenario planning

Retreats can produce a range of benefits beyond the direct outcomes of concentrated board attention to one specific topic. They provide opportunities for team building among board members, giving members the chance to increase their appreciation of one another's skills, expertise, and strengths. They can also serve as vehicles for strengthening communication and collaboration between board and staff or for allowing a divided board to air and resolve differences.

A board can exercise its authority only when it meets and makes decisions. In the boardroom, individual board members coalesce and become a board. It is in meetings that the group acts as visionary, missionary, policy maker, direction setter, overseer, and decision maker in its commitment to carry out the organization's purposes.

? QUESTIONS THE BOARD SHOULD ASK

1. Is there enough "meat" on our board's table to fully engage the talent and energy of its members?

2. What is our average attendance at board meetings? What percentage of the board participates at meetings?

3. Where can the board add value that the staff cannot provide?

4. How well do our meeting calendar and agendas correlate with our strategic plan? Is the number of meetings adequate? Are some meetings unnecessary?

5. Do our meeting agendas allocate sufficient time to relevant issues, dynamic exchanges, and full deliberation? How might we make our time together more meaningful?

6. Do our board retreats produce benefits more varied and profound than those at regular meetings?

CHAPTER 6

BOARD DYNAMICS

Successful boards focus on purposefully developing the critical elements of board leadership, composition, structure, and practices. They also pay attention to the development of individual board members and of the board as a whole. They continually strive to promote a working environment that encourages collaboration, partnership, engagement, trust, respect, flexibility, and interaction.

The board chair and the chief executive take the lead, but every board member also contributes to the overall group dynamic. Only by attending as purposefully to the development of the dynamics of the group as to the work of the group — governing — can a board hope to realize the promise of each individual member, gather individuals into a harmonious group, and harness the group's potential.

BUILDING TRUST THROUGH OPEN COMMUNICATION

Trusting relationships among the chair, the chief executive, and the members of the board compound the board's ability to fulfill its obligations — and find fulfillment in doing so. Communicating openly and often builds trust. Led by the chair, the board needs to establish regular procedures and checks to ensure that the lines of communication stay open, both within the board and between the board and the staff.

Trust among Board Members. Periodic opportunities for board members to gather informally and become better acquainted can reinforce interpersonal relationships and strengthen the lines of communication. As members come to know and understand one another and their respective values, styles, and skills, they develop trust and the ability to overcome differences in a spirit of respect and cooperation.

MECHANISMS FOR BUILDING TRUST

As the board incorporates trust in its role as the organization's representative, in its own methods of operating and in its relationship with the chief executive, it should keep the following in mind:

- Disclosing and making access easy to organizational documents describing financial and programmatic achievements are essential to gaining the public's trust.

- Transparency of processes for appointments for board positions and hiring the chief executive eliminate concerns about unfair treatment or discrimination.

- Incorporating a culture of positive dissent in the boardroom encourages board members to share opinions and accept counter-comments without turning issues into personal conflicts.

- Having regular executive sessions removes secrecy from these meetings and allows board members to openly and in confidence discuss internal issues without staff present.

- Regular KPAWN (what Keeps the President Awake at Night) meetings provide a safe, trusting environment for the chief executive to share personal and position-related challenges with the board.

- Annual chief executive performance evaluations allow for honest feedback and assessment of achievements under fair conditions if they are based on mutually agreed upon goals.

- Board self-assessment builds trust and confidence among board members as a collective effort to judge how the team is working together.

Source: "Building Trust with the Board," BoardSource Topic Paper. Available at www.boardsource.org/Knowledge.asp?ID=1.350.

Informal gatherings pave the way for healthy and spontaneous exchanges. By intentionally pairing or mixing board members of varying views and behaviors — from assigning seats at meals to discussion groups during meetings to reporting at a retreat — the governance committee can increase board members' awareness of one another's strengths and assets and consequently their ability to work together productively.

TIP

Trust is a key ingredient in the relationship between the board and the chief executive. Blind trust, however, can easily lead to the board rubber stamping ideas without proper scrutiny. "Trust but verify" remains the prudent way to structure the board–chief executive relationship.

Trust between Board and Staff. Open, ongoing communication and trusting relationships between board and staff fuel the organization's success. For the chief executive, this means regularly informing the board chair about opportunities, challenges, and problems; posing questions and offering answers; and sharing good and bad news early and openly. For the chair and the members of the board, it means conveying that the board is there to cooperate, to advise, and to set policies that are in the best interests of the organization.

When the board, the chair, and the chief executive work together in a trusting environment built on open communication, the board serves as a sounding board and source of support that encourages the chief executive to generate creative ideas, propose innovative programs, and explore promising alliances. Together, board and staff can critically evaluate options for responding to challenges, with respect for each other and with the knowledge that breakthrough ideas may arise out of healthy tension.

d recruitment work well, they result in a
rgetic, passionate leaders. Many boards
m of A-types" — people comfortable with
the direction. As quarterbacks accustomed
to leading their own teams and formulating strategy, these board
members typically thrive when given

- flexibility

- interactivity

- meaningful engagement

- robust communication

- deadlines

- tight time frames

- an emphasis on the organization's strategic plan

Of course, these talented men and women may not want to play
the quarterback position on the organization's board. They may
want to do something else when playing on another field. By
asking, not assuming, one organization learned that a new board
member — "one of the most dynamic people in the city" —
wanted to extend the mission rather than save it. Tired of being
asked to salvage organizations, she only wanted to be part of an
established "winner board." She also had no interest in chairing,
preferring to serve tirelessly on a committee.

MOVING FROM FORMING TO PERFORMING

The healthy practice of revitalizing a board by limiting members'
terms (see Chapter 2) makes a varying degree of acquaintance
with board culture inevitable. With the departure of veteran
members and officers and the election of their successors come
different dynamics. Everyone must become acquainted with one
another, and the new board members must familiarize
themselves with the board's structures, practices, habits, and
culture. In other words, the board can easily find itself
perpetually in the stage of forming.

To operate in performing mode, the board needs to intentionally counter this byproduct of planned turnover. Two ways of doing this are to capitalize on board members' assets and to provide continuous education opportunities. Both strategies have the added advantage of promoting board member engagement with the organization and its mission.

Capitalize on Assets. After conscientiously cultivating and recruiting board members whose intellectual, political, and social capital promise great returns for the organization (see Appendix III), the board loses if it leaves the intellectual capital untouched on the boardroom table. Failing to maximize the return on the investment shortchanges both the board member and the organization and stifles member creativity and enthusiasm. In contrast, sharing board members' knowledge enhances and hastens learning and improves the chances that "the board's collective brainpower will enlighten its collective mind" (*Governance as Leadership: Reframing the Work of Nonprofit Boards,* John Wiley & Sons and BoardSource, 2005).

Meaningfully engaging members is the secret to producing a high-functioning board. Matching board members early with important work connects them to the organization and its services. Active participation on committees and task forces deepens members' knowledge of the organization and the environment in which it operates, while giving them opportunities to get to know each other, become a cohesive team, and develop leadership skills for the board to tap later. Even negative circumstances, or less than perfect outcomes, have positive power on groups that work through challenges together; the shared effort builds both individual expertise and group cohesion.

The organization also benefits from tapping individual and collective intellectual assets in pursuit of mission because energy and innovation arise out of meaningful involvement with projects that make a difference. When board members have opportunities to share their talents, passions, and networks, they find board work rewarding and their commitment and involvement increase. They contribute to the organization's advance toward vision as well as reap personal satisfaction.

Educate Continuously. If the primary function of the board is to provide expertise and perspective to guide the organization and set its direction and policies, then the board itself must equip members with the knowledge, skills, and understanding to do its work. "An organization profits far more from a knowledgeable board than from a loose federation of knowledgeable trustees," note the authors of *Governance as Leadership: Reframing the Work of Nonprofit Boards* (John Wiley & Sons and BoardSource, 2005). Isolated educational segments during board meetings are not sufficient; the board must develop a culture conducive to continuous learning so that it both plans for learning and responds to learning opportunities.

Continuous learning should be formalized and become intentional not only within but also outside of board meetings. The governance committee is responsible for building and overseeing a formal framework of board member education, but the board chair–chief executive team sets the tone and supervises the framework. It may include

- reports from program staff or mini-lectures from local experts to extend board members' knowledge

- attendance at conferences to upgrade governing skills, enlarge networks, and share practices

- customized plans for board members to build individual capacity, which may include attending specialized training, leading a task force, or undertaking a task outside of a personal comfort zone

- pairing the confidence of an experienced board member with the fresh perspective of a neophyte for a special task, such as visiting an elected official

As board members deepen their knowledge of the organization, its field or industry, and its external environment, they find themselves better positioned to help the organization. By designing for continuous learning, structurally and culturally, boards produce informed decision makers, advocates, and communicators. As one board member said, "My board has retrofitted me to serve my community!"

FOSTERING DEBATE

People who serve tirelessly on nonprofit boards, regardless of how well-known they may be for their assertiveness and leadership qualities, bring generosity and concern for others to their board roles. Focused on collegiality, they may refrain from debating issues wholeheartedly when their opinions collide with a fellow member's views.

Responding to a governance committee that asked, "Why do you think it is hard for board members to ask the hard questions and speak the hard truths?" one board member observed, "People want to be accepted. They work all day and come to a board meeting to reinforce mission; they want to feel good about their work; they are looking for a sanctuary."

Such pussyfooting dampens hoped-for dialogue, innovative problem solving, and creative tension. Niceness is not a trait to purge — but a board must override it to perform dynamically. One strategy is to insert "catalytic questions" into regularly scheduled meetings or as a one-item agenda. These questions galvanize small group discussions around topics of strategic importance with reports back to whole board. They inspire board members to share opinions, experiences, and ideas spontaneously.

Examples of such questions, excerpted from *Governance as Leadership,* include

- Five years from now, what will this organization's key constituents consider the most important legacy of the current board?

- In five years, what will be different about the board or how we govern?

- What is the biggest gap between what the organization claims it is and what it actually is?

Some organizations incorporate scenario planning to capitalize on members' energy and creativity. Whether they are used to equip a board to tackle tough problems and produce results or to prepare for strategic planning, a potential merger, or some seismic shift, these techniques build a cohesive, prepared board.

TONING DOWN DISSONANCE

Most nonprofit board members tend to be compatible and cooperative, but differences of opinion and conflicts are bound to arise. When they involve critical issues and processes and are addressed with mutual respect, such conflicts are healthy for the organization. On the other hand, personal conflicts and disruptive behavior are divisive. Individual members with inappropriate personal agendas or overbearing personalities can drive away new and promising members and cause severe disorder.

The first line of defense against these predicaments occurs during the prospecting phase of recruitment, when the governance committee determines whether a potential board member has a personal agenda or an operating style that might lead to problems down the road. The committee should purposefully vet and test candidates for unqualified loyalty to the organization, the ability to set aside personal agendas, and an open attitude and respect for alternative views.

TIP

If you have a board member who always seems to be contrary and often complains about other people's work or opinions, the chair should assign this member a special task related to the issue most often complained about. This not only engages the board member in a constructive manner but also can provide the member with the opportunity to become more effective on the board.

The recruiting process does not always identify people with personal ambitions or zealous ideals who wish to use the organization for their own purposes. These people may nurture alliances and use deceptive tactics to gain power within the board.

The governance committee should present educational opportunities that deepen knowledge of the organization and promote development of skills that will support its growth and provide retreat-like situations for members to build relationships and respect for diverse styles. Such activities can encourage board members with personal agendas to recognize the ways that such agendas may subvert the organization's ability to pursue its mission. Also, the governance committee can help to counteract the imposition of personal agendas on the organization's business by conducting formal and informal board member evaluations.

The surest way to preclude destructive dissonance is to incorporate such proven practices as renewing board members' terms when their contributions align with the strategic needs, encouraging healthy debate, and offering continuous learning opportunities. In addition, working in smaller groups — during retreats and committee or task force meetings, for example — helps build relations among members. Even negative circumstances or less-than-perfect outcomes positively affect groups that work through challenges together. Sharing responsibility for the assigned task builds a growing comprehension of the scope of the organization's work and sharpens leadership skills.

QUESTIONS THE BOARD SHOULD ASK

1. How would you describe the level of trust among our board members?

2. How healthy is our board's communication with members? How — and how often — do we determine that?

3. How healthy is our board's communication with the chief executive? How do we know what challenges the chief executive faces?

4. Can we characterize our board meetings as open, honest debate? If so, what specific examples during the last year support that assessment? If not, why not?

6. Do our board retreats produce benefits more varied and profound than those at regular meetings?

CONCLUSION

TOWARD A BETTER BOARD

Good governance should be celebrated. It represents a significant achievement, one to recognize and reward. The gratification of contributing to a productive board that enables an organization to advance on its mission is reward in itself, but those responsible for making it happen deserve a medal.

SIX THINGS TO REMEMBER

In the final analysis, the formula for effective governance boils down to six essential ingredients:

1. **The mission.** A clear, concise, and compelling mission unifies and motivates the board and staff to achieve meaningful results.

2. **The leadership of the board and the organization.** Look at any high-performing organization, and you will find it led by a board chair and chief executive committed to a constructive partnership built on a shared understanding of mission and vision; reciprocal communication; and mutual respect, trust, and support for each other and the partnership.

3. **The strategic plan.** The plan charts a future course and then drives the actions that move the organization forward. It informs the board's structures, aligning committees and task forces with strategic objectives and shaping their charts of work, timetables, and checkpoints. And it guides the leadership prospecting process.

4. **The composition of the board and staff.** With the right people in the right positions, working on the right mission, success is within reach.

5. **Board meetings.** As the boardroom is the formal place where the board acts on its authority, a focused, well-planned, and effectively executed meeting is the crux of decision making.

6. **A streamlined structure.** When aligned with the strategic priorities of the organization, an efficient structure allows board and staff to apply their skills in concert to fulfill the mission.

This formula is neither complex nor profound, but few organizations apply it consistently or thoroughly. Those that do find that, while effective governance takes time, flexibility, intention, and attention, it makes all the difference in the world to the nonprofit organization and to the community it serves.

APPENDIX I

SAMPLE JOB DESCRIPTIONS

THE BOARD CHAIR

POSITION SUMMARY

The board chair is the senior volunteer leader of XYZ Organization and presides at all meetings of the board of directors, the executive committee, and other meetings as required.

KEY RESPONSIBILITIES

Policy and planning. Works with the chief executive and the board to establish the guiding principles, policies, and mission for the organization — for example, by initiating a regular review of the organization's strategic plan and mission to keep them fresh and relevant and by establishing metrics to measure success.

Budget and finances. Works with the appropriate board members to oversee the budget of the organization and ensures that the board assumes ultimate responsibility for the integrity of the organization's finances.

Board meetings. Leads and facilitates board meetings by making sure that the agenda is closely followed, that every board member has the opportunity to participate in discussions, and that the board uses proper decision-making procedures.

Board committees. Serves as an ad hoc member of all board committees and works to structure a committee system that contributes to the board's overall effectiveness.

Board development. Oversees efforts to build and maintain a strong board — by setting goals and expectations for the board, cultivating leadership among individual board members, and working with the governance committee to make board development a priority.

Board recruitment and orientation. Works with the governance committee to identify and recruit new board members who bring important skills and knowledge to the board.

Board evaluation. Works to make sure the board has opportunities to reflect regularly on how well it is meeting its responsibilities to the organization — in part by overseeing a board self-assessment every three years.

Staff oversight, compensation, and evaluation. Oversees the hiring, evaluation, and compensation of the chief executive. Also ensures the development of a succession plan for the chief executive's position — for example, by making sure that other staff have the capabilities needed to lead the organization.

Fundraising. Guides the work of the board to secure funds for the organization by

- overseeing the development of fundraising policies

- encouraging and supporting the fundraising efforts of the development committee and individual board members

- soliciting contributions from board members and selected outside contributors

- setting an example by contributing personally to the organization

Public relations and communication. Speaks for the board in the event of a controversy or crisis; oversees the development of communication policies; and works to promote the work of the organization in conversations, speeches, interviews, and other day-to-day activities.

THE CHIEF EXECUTIVE

POSITION SUMMARY

The chief executive is responsible for the overall administration and management of XYZ Organization, including service programs, fundraising, and business operations.

KEY RESPONSIBILITIES

Policy and planning. Develops policies and guidelines for consideration by the board; works with the staff to carry out the XYZ mission and implement the strategic plan; and provides administrative support for the board's policymaking activities.

Budget and finances. Proposes budgets to the board and manages organizational programs and finances according to board-adopted financial policies and budget guidelines.

Board meetings. Works with the board chair to prepare the agenda for board meetings; ensures that board members have good and concise information and meeting materials; participates actively in board meetings as appropriate.

Board committees. Attends appropriate committee meetings and makes sure committees have the staff support and the information they need to do their jobs.

Board development. Works closely with the board chair and committee leaders to put together programs and activities that nurture future board leaders while keeping all board members engaged in the work of the organization.

Board recruitment and orientation. Participates in board recruitment by helping to identify, cultivate, and recruit new board members, as appropriate, and by working with committee leaders to structure board orientations.

Board evaluation. Works closely with the chair and the governance committee to create an evaluation process that provides useful information and helps the board do a better job.

Staff oversight, compensation, and evaluation. Oversees the work of all staff, evaluates staff performance, and oversees salary decisions.

Fundraising. Coordinates the organization's overall fundraising effort while personally soliciting potential major donors, frequently in partnership with the board chair and other appropriate board members.

Public relations and communication. Serves as the official spokesperson for the organization, oversees the organization's official public relations and communication program, and supports board members' public relations efforts, as appropriate.

APPENDIX II

SAMPLE COMMITTEE DOCUMENTS

Nonprofit organizations that find the following samples helpful may adapt the documents to their own structure and culture.

SAMPLE #1: GOVERNANCE COMMITTEE COMMISSION

STATEMENT OF PURPOSE

The constitution of the XYZ Organization (Article V. Sec. 3.) calls for the board to appoint a Governance Committee to "train board members in their work and the work of the organization; to assess board needs for new member qualities and skills; to assess board member performance; and to identify, cultivate, recruit, and nominate individuals to serve as members of the board."

The expected outcome from the work of this committee will be to ensure an effective board by guaranteeing that the board

- takes responsibility for its own development, learning, and behavior

- intentionally sets and enforces its own expectations

- allots time, attention, and resources to learning about stewardship of intellectual capital, building and maintaining relationships that matter, understanding the competitive environment, and thinking strategically

COMMITTEE COMPOSITION

Chaired by a member of the board, staffed by a member of the executive office, plus five to seven volunteer members with a variety of expertise and connections. Committee members must be capable of

- maintaining confidences

- objectively evaluating peers and confronting lackluster participation by colleagues

- identifying, cultivating, and evaluating prospects

- bringing a positive, constructive attitude and well-developed emotional intelligence to work with the board

- demonstrating an eagerness to become expert in high-impact governance

- assuming accountability for developing the board as a resource

COMMISSION

The committee is commissioned to develop the board by focusing on

Roles and Responsibilities

- Lead the board in regularly reviewing and updating the board's statement of its role and areas of responsibility and the expectations of individual board members.

- Assist the board in periodically updating and clarifying the primary areas of focus for the board — the board's agenda for the next year or two, based on the strategic plan.

- Ensure the committee structure is designed to accomplish strategic work of XYZ Organization as well provide high-impact governance.

Board Composition

- Lead in assessing current and anticipated needs for board composition, determining the board's knowledge, attributes, skills, abilities, influence, and access the board will need to consider to accomplish its strategic and future work.

- Develop a profile of the board as determined by strategic goals and objectives.

- Identify, cultivate, evaluate, and recruit candidates for board service.

- In cooperation with the board chair, meet annually with each board member to assess continuing interest in board membership and term of service.

- Work with each board member to identify the appropriate role that individual might assume on behalf of the organization.

Knowledge

- Design and oversee a process of board orientation, to include providing information prior to election as a board member and when needed during the first cycle of board activity for new board members.

- Design and implement an ongoing program of board information and education.

Effectiveness

- Lead the periodic assessment of the board's performance. Propose, as appropriate, changes in board structure, roles, and responsibilities.

- Provide ongoing counsel to the board chair and other board leaders on steps to take to enhance board effectiveness.

- Regularly review the board's practices regarding member participation, conflict of interest, confidentiality, etc., and suggest improvements as needed.

- Periodically review and update the board's policy guidelines and practices.

Leadership

- Ensure the board has a succession plan, supporting efforts to prepare for future board leadership.

- Support leadership development of board members for election as board officers as needed.

SAMPLE #2: ROLES OF COMMITTEE CHAIRS AND MEMBERS

ROLE OF COMMITTEE CHAIRS

- Set the tone for committee work, ensure that members have the information they need to do their jobs, and oversee the logistics of the committee's operation.

- Assign work to committee members, set meeting agendas, run meetings, and ensure distribution of minutes and reports to members.

- As the committee's link to the board, frequently consult with and report to the board chair.

- Report to the full board on committee decisions, policy recommendations, and other committee business.

- Work closely with the chief executive and other staff liaisons to the committee.

- Initiate and lead the committee's annual evaluation. Through this process, committee members review their accomplishments in relation to committee goals and reflect on areas of the committee's work that need improvement.

ROLE OF COMMITTEE MEMBERS

- Make a serious commitment to participate actively in the committee's work, including substantive participation in meetings and discussions.

- Volunteer for and willingly accept assignments and complete them thoroughly and on time.

- Stay informed about committee matters, prepare well for meetings, and review and comment on minutes and reports.

- Get to know other committee members and build a collegial working relationship that contributes to consensus.

- Actively participate in the committee's annual evaluation.

SAMPLE #3: BOARD AGENDA TOPIC TEMPLATE

The Project Management Institute (PMI) uses this template to streamline the presentation and ensure the consistency of items requiring board action. Readers who want to reprint or customize the following template should contact PMI for permission at www.pmi.org.

Agenda Topic:

Date Submitted:

Name of Board Standing Committee or Individual Submitting Agenda Topic:

Name of Board Director Presenting the Agenda Topic:

Type of Item Information; Discussion; Motion; Motion Resulting in a Change to a Governing Document

Identify the Board's Work **Domain:** Board Building; Business, Fiduciary; Strategic

Board Vote Required:

1. Motion(s) or Other Outcome(s) for Board deliberation and decision. Any proposed change to a governing document must be included in the motion *(The Action):* (Any approved motions that result in a change to a governing document are deemed perpetual unless otherwise changed in a subsequent Board-approved motion. All other motions approving an action will be effective for 12 months from the date of approval, unless otherwise specified.)

2. State the issue and the context and background surrounding the issue, including anything the Board has already said about this issue through formal motions, governing documents, or the strategic plan *(Situational Analysis/Background):*

3. What impact does this issue have for PMI stakeholders? What do we know about the needs, wants, and views of PMI stakeholders relevant to this issue? Include specific supporting information, current realities, and evolving dynamics *(Stakeholder's Perspective):*

4. Business Analysis *(Cultural, Legal, Financial, and Impact Analysis)*: Please respond to each of the following questions.

- What, if any, strategic threats or opportunities might result?

- What, if any, are the legal/ethical implications associated with this proposal? Has a legal/ethical review been completed?

- Describe how financial and other necessary resources, i.e., human, IT, etc., required to implement the proposal or other outcomes have been identified and allocated.

- Describe any cultural or regional concerns or opportunities that might arise.

- State if any other viable options or alternatives for the proposal or other outcomes exist.

5. Attachment(s)/Reference(s) *(Supporting Information)*:

6. Proposed Communication Plan and Potential Action Items *(Necessary Follow-up)*:
- Was a communication plan developed?

- What are the milestones for the plan and who is responsible for each?

- Are there any considerable risks (positive or negative) that exist when communications are released about this action?

- If so, what are they and how are they to be handled?

© 2008 Project Management Institute, Inc. All rights reserved. Reprinted with permission.

APPENDIX III

SAMPLE GRID FOR EVALUATING BOARD CAPITAL

According to Chait, Ryan, and Taylor, in their book *Governance as Leadership,* "A board contributes various types of capital and then invests those resources in the governance of the institution, ideally at a favorable rate of return." With that idea in mind, developing a spreadsheet or chart, such as the one below, enables the governance committee to better understand the various types of capital provided by the current board and identify areas where new board members could be most beneficial. You might also develop a color coding system for filling out the grid, for example

Strong Positive (Blue)

Positive (Green)

Neutral (Yellow)

Negative (Red)

	NAME A	NAME B	NAME C	NAME D
TERM COMPLETES	2009	2009	2010	2010
Intellectual Capital				
Hard Skills				
Insurance				

	NAME A	NAME B	NAME C	NAME D
TERM COMPLETES	2009	2009	2010	2010
Accounting				
Investment				
Legal				
Real Estate				
Architecture				
Soft Skills				
Strategic Planning				
Leadership Transition				
Financial Development				
Reputational Capital				
Marketing Expertise				
Efforts to Build XYZ Brand				
Length of Service to XYZ				

	NAME A	NAME B	NAME C	NAME D
TERM COMPLETES	2009	2009	2010	2010
Reputation outside of XYZ				
Other Traits (Diversity)				
Age				
Gender				
Race				
Disability				
Geography				
Political Capital				
Government Connections				
Media Connections				
Willingness to Use Capital as a Board Member				
Level of Interaction with Staff				
Interaction with XYZ Affiliates				

	NAME A	NAME B	NAME C	NAME D
TERM COMPLETES	2009	2009	2010	2010
Social Capital				
Interaction Quality w/other Board Members				
Willingness to Disagree				
Willingness to Assume Responsibility				
Performance on Committees				
Monetary Capital				
Historical Giving Patterns				
Financial Position				

APPENDIX IV

SAMPLE BOARD MEETING EVALUATION

	OK	NEEDS IMPROVEMENT
1. The agenda was clear, supported by the necessary documents, and circulated prior to the meeting.		
2. All board members came prepared to discuss the materials sent in advance.		
3. Reports were clear and contained needed information.		
4. We avoided getting into administrative/management details.		
5. A diversity of opinions was expressed, and issues were dealt with in a respectful manner.		
6. The chair guided the meeting effectively.		
7. Members participated responsibly.		
8. Next steps were identified and responsibilities assigned.		
9. All board members were present.		
10. The meeting began and ended on time.		
11. The meeting room was conducive to work.		
12. We enjoyed being together.		

SUGGESTIONS FOR IMPROVEMENT

SUGGESTED RESOURCES

Axelrod, R. Nancy R. *Chief Executive Succession Planning.* Washington, DC: BoardSource, 2002.

How ready are you for a leadership transition? In *Chief Executive Succession Planning,* author Nancy R. Axelrod explains why it is important for your board to have a leadership transition plan whether or not you anticipate an upcoming executive search. Learn how to devise an ongoing chief executive officer succession plan that is linked to the strategic planning, mission, and vision of your organization. Help your board prepare for the future by tying the needs of the organization into the chief executive officer job description and chief executive officer evaluation.

BoardSource. *The Source: Twelve Principles of Governance That Power Exceptional Boards.* Washington, DC: BoardSource, 2005.

With the publication in 2005 of *The Source: Twelve Principles of Governance That Power Exceptional Boards,* BoardSource issued a call to action for nonprofit boards: Make a discernable difference in your organization by moving from passive stewardship to active leadership. Your board can move from being a responsible board to being an exceptional board that adds significant value to your organization and its advance on mission just as these boards have done.

Bobowick, Marla J., Sandra R. Hughes, and Berit M.Lakey, *Transforming Board Structure: Strategies for Committees and Task Forces.* Washington, DC: BoardSource, 2001.

Committees provide an opportunity for board members to use their expertise and work together on specific projects, while allowing the board to keep its attention on the big picture. It is easy, however, for committee structure to become complicated and ineffective. Boards with too many standing committees may find their resources spread too thin and that the work of the full board is repeating that of individual committees.

Transforming Board Structure is an introductory publication for the BoardSource Committee Series. In this essential resource, the authors provide a fresh look at committees and illustrate how boards can use simple and flexible work groups to streamline the work of the full board.

Chait, Richard P., William P. Ryan, and Barbara E. Taylor *Governance as Leadership: Reframing the Work of Nonprofit Boards.* Hoboken, NJ: John Wiley & Sons, 2005.

Written by noted consultants and researchers Richard P. Chait, William P. Ryan, and Barbara E. Taylor, *Governance as Leadership* redefines nonprofit governance. It provides a powerful framework for a new covenant between trustees and executives: more macrogovernance in exchange for less micromanagement. This book sheds new light on the traditional fiduciary and strategic work of the board and introduces a critical third dimension of effective trusteeship: generative governance. It serves boards as both a resource of fresh approaches to familiar territory and a lucid guide to important new territory, and provides a road map that leads nonprofit trustees and executives to governance as leadership.

Flynn, Outi. *Meet Smarter: A Guide to Better Nonprofit Board Meetings.* Washington, DC: BoardSource, 2004.

Efficient board meetings are not difficult to achieve. Whether you're new to the boardroom or an old pro, you'll find ready-to-use information that will improve the efficiency of your meetings. *Meet Smarter* provides practical solutions to better meetings, explanations of the legal framework, and process practices that will reinvigorate your board meetings. With a detailed table of contents, this book is a must-have reference guide for nonprofit chief executives, board members, organizational staff, and any other participant in key meetings of the board.

Herman, Robert D., and Richard D.Heimovics, *Executive Leadership in Nonprofit Organizations: New Starts for Shaping Board-Staff Dynamics*. San Francisco: Jossey-Bass, 1991.

This classic describes the strategies that effective executives use to position their organizations in the larger environment and offers detailed guidance on how executives can work more productively with their boards.

Hopkins, Bruce R. *Legal Responsibilities of Nonprofit Boards, Second Edition*. Washington, DC: BoardSource, 2009.

All board members should understand their legal responsibilities, including when and how they can be held personally liable and what type of oversight they should provide. Discover the essential information that board members should know to protect themselves and their organization. Written in nontechnical language, the *Legal Responsibilities of Nonprofit Boards* by Bruce R. Hopkins provides legal concepts and definitions, as well as a detailed discussion on ethics.

Lakey, Berit M. *The Board Building Cycle, Second Edition*. Washington, DC: BoardSource, 2007.

Good boards do not just happen: They take care, thought, and planning. The second edition of this bestseller features nine steps for your board to follow through the board development process, including identifying, cultivating, and recruiting prospective board members; orienting new board members; encouraging board members to become more active; educating the board about the organization's work and context; rotating out board members to make room for new skills and insights; engaging the board in a self-evaluation; and celebrating the board's victories and successes.

Lakey, Berit M. *Nonprofit Governance: Steering Your Organization with Authority and Accountability.* Washington, DC: BoardSource, 2000.

Universities, hospitals, environmental organizations, and human services organizations — while each may be run differently, all nonprofit boards have the authority to decide the organization's direction and they are accountable for how this authority is carried out.

Nonprofit Governance: Steering Your Organization with Authority and Accountability takes an innovative look at governance and describes ways that boards and board members can add value to the organizations they serve.

Written by BoardSource governance consultant Berit M. Lakey, this book defines the difference between governance and management and outlines how nonprofit boards carry out the charge to set direction, ensure the necessary resources, and provide oversight.

Lakey, Berit M., Sandra R. Hughes, and Outi Flynn. *Governance Committee.* Washington, DC: BoardSource, 2004.

All things must be properly fed and cared for in order to thrive and succeed. A nonprofit board is no different. The governance committee ensures the constant health and effectiveness of the full board and the work it performs for the organization. It expands the traditional idea of a nominating committee, clarifying the variety of responsibilities a governance committee truly has.

McLaughlin, Thomas A. *Financial Committees.* Washington, DC: BoardSource, 2004.

With the recent, ongoing changes in regulations and accountability standards, understanding the financial roles and responsibilities of a nonprofit board is absolutely necessary. *Financial Committees,* confirms the need for skilled and experienced committee members in dealing with both board-related and organizational fiscal matters. The guidelines provided in this book will help the reader understand how to best configure financial committees depending on the size and available resources of the board.

Moyers, Richard L. *The Nonprofit Chief Executive's Ten Basic Responsibilities*. Washington, DC: BoardSource, 2006.

Many chief executives can find guidebooks or practical tools to improve their skills as supervisors, communicators, and program managers. But most chief executives also want to have a greater understanding of their responsibilities in the context of their partnership with the board, and have fewer places to turn.

The Nonprofit Chief Executive's Ten Basic Responsibilities seeks to fill that hole. It discusses all the chief executive's responsibilities, including supervising staff, overseeing operations, and supporting the board. The 10 sections acknowledge the breadth and complexity of the chief executive's role, and can serve as benchmarks and guideposts for those chief executives who want to explore specific aspects of their responsibilities in greater depth.

Page, Scott. *The Difference: How the Power of Diversity Creates Better Groups, Firms, Schools, and Societies*. Princeton, NJ: Princeton University Press, 2007.

In this landmark book, Scott Page redefines the way we understand ourselves in relation to one another. *The Difference* is about how we think in groups — and how our collective wisdom exceeds the sum of its parts. Why can teams of people find better solutions than brilliant individuals working alone? And why are the best group decisions and predictions those that draw upon the very qualities that make each of us unique? The answers lie in diversity — not what we look like outside, but what we look like within, our distinct tools and abilities.

Panel on the Nonprofit Sector. *Principles for Good Governance and Ethical Practice: A Guide for Charities and Foundations.* October 2007.

Principles for Good Governance represents the first time that charities and foundations reflecting a broad cross-section of the American nonprofit community have come together to develop principles of ethical conduct, accountability, and transparency that they aspire to and encourage all organizations to follow. The Guide outlines 33 practices designed to support board members and staff leaders of every charitable organization as they work to improve their own operations.

Taylor, Barbara E., Richard P. Chait, and Thomas Holland. "The New Work of the Nonprofit Board" *Harvard Business Review,* September/October 1996.

In 1996, Barbara Taylor, Richard Chait, and Thomas Holland proposed a radically new way to look at the board's structure and their concept is still reverberating in the boardrooms. The classic paper is based on what matters most as a guide for the board. To add value, the board should help provide opportunities for the chief executive to bounce off ideas on issues of importance, develop mechanisms for effective oversight, rely on new methods to alleviate resistance to change, and itself model the behavior it wants to see implemented into the culture of the organization.

Tuckman, Bruce W. "Developmental Sequence in Small Groups," *Psychological Bulletin* 63, 1965.

Group leaders often make reference to "the stages of group development" and these stages — forming, storming, norming, and performing — were proposed by Bruce Tuckman in 1965 based on his examination of empirical research studies. In this classic article, we find a rich description of these stages under a variety of settings as well as their applicability to both group structure and task activity.

Wertheimer, Mindy R. *The Board Chair Handbook, Second Edition.* Washington, DC: BoardSource, 2007.

Whether you are a seasoned board chair wanting to brush up and learn something new, an incoming board chair seeking knowledge and skills, or a person considering the possibility of becoming a board chair, this definitive and newly revised guide provides the blueprint for being successful and effective in your leadership role. User friendly and practical, this book focuses on the roles and responsibilities of the board chair position, addresses the all-important work partnership with the organization's chief executive, and outlines the solid communications skills that the board chair's work requires — skills that invite dialogue in a nonjudgmental, respectful atmosphere. Accompanying materials provide sample agendas, letters, and job descriptions to help you do your job effectively.

ABOUT THE AUTHORS

CHARLES F. (CHIC) DAMBACH

Chic Dambach is president and chief executive officer of the Alliance for Peacebuilding, a global network of organizations devoted to reducing the frequency and severity of violent conflicts. Previous chief executive positions include the Operation Respect, National Peace Corps Association, Museum Trustee Association, and National Assembly of Local Arts Agencies. He has been a senior consultant with BoardSource and continues to speak at conferences and consult with nonprofit organizations on effective governance.

His governing board experience includes the Coalition for American Leadership Abroad (chair), US Canoe and Kayak Team (chair), Pan American Canoe Federation (president), Baltimore CityLit (chair), Global Partnership for the Prevention of Armed Conflict, J. William and Harriet Fulbright Center, CARE, InterAction, International Development Conference, and American Canoe Association.

Dambach is the co-author of *The Business Professional's Guide to Nonprofit Board Service.* His articles have appeared in *Foreign Service Journal, Social Education, Board Member, WorldView,* and *Olympian.* He has been featured in the *Christian Science Monitor* and the German news magazine *Focus,* as well as the alumni magazines of both Oklahoma State University and Wake Forest University. He was named the Distinguished Alumnus for 2004 by the Oklahoma State University College of Arts and Sciences. In 2001, he received the International Platform Association's Global Coalition Peace Award.

MELISSA DAVIS

Melissa Davis was the director of National Governance at the YMCA of the USA until leaving Chicago in 2007 to pursue a master's degree in Buddhist Studies from the University of Hong Kong.

Davis worked with the YMCA for more than 30 years as both a volunteer and staff member. Before joining the YMCA of the USA in 1997 as associate director for volunteer development, she was vice president for community relations at The Community YMCA in Red Bank, New Jersey, and executive director of its newly incorporated foundation. During her tenure at Y-USA, she staffed the task force that designed the governance system for the national office of the YMCA and headed the Knowledge Publishing department.

She has chaired the Lake Champlain Committee, a New York/Vermont advocacy board; served as a trustee of the smallest chartered library in New York; drafted the founding bylaws for the Asbury Park Consortium; and served as the first female on the board of a national bank located in upstate New York. In addition, she has authored, reviewed, and contributed to books and articles on nonprofit governance and volunteer practices.

Davis holds a bachelor's degree in linguistics from Georgetown University, a master's degree in liberal arts from the University of Chicago, and a master's degree in Buddhist Studies from the University of Hong Kong.

ROBERT L. GALE

Robert L. Gale is president emeritus of the Association of Governing Boards of Universities and Colleges (AGB), a national association that he served as president for 18 years. Prior to his appointment to AGB, he was founder, chairman of the board, and chief executive officer of Gale Associates, Inc., a consulting firm that worked with more than 100 nonprofit organizations. He also served as vice president of his alma mater, Carleton College, and as the first director of recruiting and then director of public affairs for the Peace Corps. In addition, he was one of the first staff members of the Equal Employment Opportunity Commission, where he served as director of public affairs.

Gale secured grants of $1.2 million to found the National Center for Nonprofit Boards, now BoardSource, and served as a board member. Over the years, he has served on more than 40 other nonprofit boards, including Carleton College, the University of Pretoria Fund, The National Executive Service Corps, the Wilson Foundation, the National Peace Garden Foundation (chair), Fund for America, the National Peace Corps Association, and the Washington Urban League, where he served on the board for 25 years.

ACKNOWLEDGMENTS

The authors wish to thank the following people for providing many of the examples in this book:

Nancy Axelrod, Principal, Nonprofit Leadership Services; Clark Baker, President/CEO, YMCA of Greater Houston; Merv Bennett, President/CEO, YMCA of the Pikes Peak Region; Barb Bettin, President/CEO, YMCA of Lincoln; Cathi Duchon, President, Ann Arbor YMCA; Lori Fisher, Executive Director, Lake Champlain Committee; Ted Cornell, Chair, Wadhams Free Library; Nancy Fuhrman, Vice President Consulting, Executive Service Corps of Chicago; Lew Gedansky, Director, Governance and Executive Programs, Project Management Institute; Seth Goldman, Metro 30 Resource Director, YMCA of the USA; Scott Haldane, President/CEO, YMCA of Greater Toronto; Lourdes Hernandez, YMCA of Metropolitan Los Angeles; Jack Lund, CEO, YMCA of Greater New York; Neil Nicoll, President/CEO, YMCA of the USA; Ben Rikkers, Associate, Foley & Lardner; and Larry Rosen, President/CEO, YMCA of Metropolitan Los Angeles.